FIRST YOU SHAVE
Your head

*

FIRST YOU SHAVE

your head

G E R I   L A R K I N

CELESTIAL**ARTS**
Berkeley, California

CELESTIALARTS

P.O. Box 7123
Berkeley, California 94707

Distributed in Canada by Ten Speed Canada, in the United Kingdom and Europe by Airlift Books, in New Zealand by Tandem Press, in Australia by Simon & Schuster Australia, in South Africa by Real Books, and in Singapore, Malaysia, Hong Kong, and Thailand by Berkeley Books.

Cover and text design by Greene Design
Cover photograph by PhotoDisc

Library of Congress Cataloging-in-Publication Data

Larkin, Geraldine A.
   First you shave your head / Geri Larkin.
      p. cm.
   ISBN 1-58761-009-4 (alk. paper)
   1. Buddhist pilgrims and pilgrimages--Korea (South) 2. Temples, Buddhist--Korea (South) 3. Korea (South)--Description and travel. 4. Korea (South)--Social life and customs. I. Title.

BQ6350 .L37 2001
294.3'44'092--dc21
[B]

                                        2001042238

First printing, 2001
Printed in the Canada

1 2 3 4 5 — 05 04 03 02 01

Dedication

This book is dedicated to Jamie Elizabeth Markus.
She willed my survival.

Acknowledgements

Thank yous: Thank you Sunim. Thank you Haju. Thank you Kaeo. Thank you to all the monks and nuns who housed and fed us. Thank you to the comfort women and the posalnims who did what they could. Thank you Andrea. Over and over. Thank you Veronica. Thank you family. Thank you to my friends in the ten directions. Thank you Buddha. Thank you Sangha. Thank you dharma. I bow to the ground in gratitude.

Contents

Preface xi

Chapter One: **Why Me, Buddha?** 1

Chapter Two: **Why Korea?** 7
Items Packed for the Pilgrimage
The Itinerary as Best I Remember

Chapter Three: **On Korean Soil : A Juicy Beginning** 23

Chapter Four: **The Pattern of Our Days** 35

Chapter Five: **Into the Mountains** 51

Chapter Six: **Tongdosa and Beyond** 61

Chapter Seven: **Just This** 79

Chapter Eight: **Climbing the Mountains in Typhoons Practice** . . 99

Chapter Nine: **G. I. P'arang** 109

Chapter Ten: **Clarity and Compassion Care of Korea** 125

Chapter Eleven: **P'arang Sunim** 141

Chapter Twelve: **Pleas from the Mountains** 147

Preface

✳

This book is about a pilgrimage to Korea to meet Zen masters tucked in the mountains, surrounded by Buddhist culture. I got to go because my dharma sister, Haju Sunim, was named heir to our teacher, Venerable Samu Sunim. He was taking her to Korea and, frankly, she needed the company of another woman.

All pilgrimages are life-changing experiences. The surprise is always how our lives change coming home. Sometimes wonderful. Sometimes excruciatingly painful. Sometimes both. It's all okay.

I pulled the book from memory and two journals I kept on the trip. It's as true as I know how to be. As some famous person (or was it my mother?) once said, "This is my truth and I'm sticking to it."

Bow.

P'arang Geri Larkin
May 13, 2001

"Of course, the deep penetrative meditation of the Teaching and Entry into the Stream...is open to all. Some may be fit to approach it because of their karmic inheritance, but intense and sustained application is required, and so efforts of this kind are usually reserved for the cloister. The Way is indeed gradual but there is a 'fast gradual' and a 'slow gradual.'

The 'fast gradual' is the rapid cure of the man wounded by the arrow. It consists of the removal of the arrow and the closing of the wound. The nature of the process can be painful, and it is best performed in the ideal circumstances of a sterilized opening theater. The 'fast gradual' or rapid cure was regarded...as the province of one under close instruction."

(*Fundamentals of Mainstream Buddhism* by Eric Cheetham. Charles E. Tuttle, Boston, 1994, p. 137-138)

The Buddhist Precepts

1. Do not harm but cherish all life.

2. Do not take what is not given but respect the things of others.

3. Do not engage in sexual promiscuity but practice purity of mind and self-restraint.

4. Do not lie but speak the truth.

5. Do not partake in the production and transaction of firearms and chemical poisons that are injurious to public health and safety, nor of drugs or liquors that confuse or weaken the mind.

6. Do not waste but conserve energy and natural resources.

7. Do not harbor enmity against others but promote peace and justice through nonviolent means.

8. Do not cling to things that belong to us but practice generosity and the joy of sharing.

Chapter One

Why Me, Buddha?

Journal entry: July 4, 1999, Ann Arbor

"I can't believe this! Sunim was meeting with the dharma students and suddenly announced that he would be going on a pilgrimage to Korea at the end of August. He wants to take Haju. Just as I was feeling the slightest twinge of jealousy starting to climb up my spine (okay, it was more than a twinge) he looked straight at me and said, "P'arang come with us. I'll pay. You just bring your body-mind." Oh my God! I *have* to go! This is such an opportunity! Thirty days of practice—just practice—plus I'll get to see what fully enlightened masters are really like. I bet they're wild. On the other hand it just occurred to me that I might have to shave my head just when I'm finally learning to French braid my hair without help. I wonder if Sunim would just let me get a buzz cut, sort of like [Susan Powter] before she disappeared from public view."

Here was the offer. I'd get to spend a month in some of the most beautiful mountains Mother Earth has to offer. Big mountains. Like Alps, only covered to the top with trees and more birds than I've ever seen in my life. Craggy in some parts, with rushing streams and rivers and waterfalls and breathtaking lookouts.

Plus I'd get to stay in mostly ancient temples and hermitages more than a thousand years old. Some of them would be built right into the sides of the mountains, with boulders for walls; temples built stone by stone and with wood local women carried on their heads up the mountains; temples that monks took hundreds of years to build—a drop in the bucket in Buddhist time.

I'd get to stay in rooms next to the monks, attend their chanting services, and eat their wholesome vegan (yuck!) meals. For some of the monks I would be the first Westerner they would see face to face—definitely the first Western woman. And, I could interview some of the old, old monks, the masters, the enlightened ones about their own experiences of living the spiritual life. I could ask them for advice, for blessings.

In return I needed to be willing to make some of my own commitments. I'd need to get by with no more than four to five hours of sleep each night and to keep silence outside of the interviews. I'd be wearing the same clothing—literally—every day and night for thirty days. (It would keep my backpack light.) No body washing unless it was a bathing day, and we would have three of those. I needed to be willing to carry all of my own gear plus some of Sunim's (about twenty pounds of his books), and I'd be climbing some of the mountains on foot since there wouldn't be roads and in Keds, because my shoes had to be leather free.

I said yes.

* * *

I met Venerable Samu Sunim twelve years ago. Having taught meditation in Canada, New York, and Michigan for more than ten years, he was the driving force behind the Zen Buddhist seminary in Ann Arbor where I spent three years prior to my own ordination. Over the years he had become a great teacher to me—wise and funny, strict and bellowing, sometimes kind, sometimes a tiger. On July 3, 1999, Sunim formally named my friend and dharma sister Haju Sukha Linda Murray as his dharma heir, formally marking her as the seventy-first generation of designated carriers of the teachings of Shakyamuni Buddha. A clumsy metaphor would go something like this: Let's say you've been going to a local Catholic Church where a quiet, humble, always sweet priest has been keeping things going for the last fifteen years. Suddenly he's been named a cardinal. In addition he's been identified as the heir apparent to the pope. It's a big deal. Not that big deals matter to Buddhists.

The dharma heir ceremony was softly beautiful. The meditation hall was a cavern of a room with a deep blue and green ceiling and orangey gold walls protected by three massive statues at one end. That day it was filled to the brim with people who know Sukha—relatives, friends, students, her dharma family. We chanted for her and with her. Describing Sukha as "an ordinary Buddha," someone whose practice is constant and whose humility marks her deep determination to serve others, Sunim gave her a carved horse-hair teaching stick to mark the occasion and read a poem extolling her efforts.

We cried. It was too moving to do anything else.

Several weeks earlier Sunim had announced in a meeting with several students making their way through the Maitreya Buddhist Seminary that he was going on a pilgrimage in the fall. More specifically, he was going to Korea, into the mountains to the old monasteries, and taking Sukha, now named Haju, with him to introduce her to the masters. I remember thinking how wonderful that would be for her and how lucky she was to be spending time walking through the mountains of South Korea, meeting with ancient Zen monks as Sunim's dharma heir—and a Western woman to boot.

When Sunim invited me to go along one might think that I would be swept away by emotion, stunned at my good fortune, tears of gratitude streaming down my face. Such an opportunity! The once in a lifetime kind. Heck, once in many lifetimes. A chance to travel on foot with not one but two Zen masters, both direct lineage holders, both English speaking. A chance to see the inner workings of Buddhism in Asia—in Korea—where the monasteries are reported to look exactly the way they did 1,000 years ago and are run like they were 1,000 years ago.

You would think.

Instead I looked at Sunim. I figured I already had a sense of what most of the rules of the road would be. Curious about his utter lack of commentary about hair I just had to ask the question.

"Do I have to shave my head?"

"Yes."

Attachments die hard. There were three months between Sunim's announcement and our departure for Korea. I spent the time obsessing about hair, looking at every fashion magazine the Ann Arbor Public Library had on its shelves, studying short hair cuts, staring at the models' faces trying to see if they were happy with their looks.

Hair matters in our society. If it didn't we wouldn't be spending billions of dollars on hair products each year—$35 billion worldwide according to the United States Bureau of Labor. In the United States that breaks down to somewhere between $300 and $400 per person. I have spent thousands. For a person who is not naturally svelte with good features such as a small nose and luscious mouth, hair matters even more. I have a big nose. Maybe the longest in my birth family. So hair has historically been one of my best features. Since long hair also matters on this Mars meets Venus landscape, it has also been long. And I admit it—but only here—the natural sun streaks that historically made me an almost strawberry blonde have been maintained with the help of "Sun In" for maybe twenty years.

Not having hair was going to be a very big deal.

There is a teaching in Tibetan Buddhism that once one's mind has stabilized in "calmly abiding," obstacles to discovering our enlightened hearts will dissipate. First anger and delusion will go. Then desire. But desire can take a long long time to loosen its grip. I was living that one out loud. I desired a head of hair, preferably one with thick wavy tendrils.

Having said all this, I did want to go to Korea.

After a couple of weeks of cutting out pictures from magazines I purchased because they had the best short-haired models, a strategy surfaced. To ease my way into baldness I would first cut my hair fashionably short. Telling myself this was no big deal I took my three favorite short-hair pictures (which I had been carrying around in my wallet) to one of the world's most talented hair cutters, in the Midwest anyway. When I told her I had decided to cut my hair she nodded and pulled all of my shoulder-length hair into a pony tail that looked like a fountain growing straight out of my scalp. And with one cut of her scissors it was gone and I looked sort of like Leonardo di Caprio. Slightly older, slightly more female.

I stumbled home and managed to refrain from looking in any mirrors or even windows. I knew I had a radically different look because I had walked right past people I've known for years and they didn't even notice me. (That part was sort of fun.) At the same time I began to notice that a lot of women had short hair and they seemed to be just fine. Even so, shaving my head was going to be a different story. I started forewarning clients that the next time they saw me I would have really, really short hair. And I kept trying to negotiate a compromise with Sunim. Would it be okay to just get a buzz cut? No. How about almost, but not quite shaved? You know…where there is still some color on your scalp that isn't flesh? I figured if he said yes I'd figure out how to do it. Another no.

Finally, surrender. A pilgrimage is a pilgrimage. If I was going to be a card-carrying Buddhist pilgrim then I had to peel my fingers off of my last scrap of identity—my hair. So I did. I just let go of me. Or so I told myself.

I'd like to tell you that facing a bald head prepared me for the trip that followed. It didn't. But it did aim me in the right direction. It was my first clue that travelling with Zen masters means learning to trust yourself and the wisdom of your own heart, so you'll know what to do, when; so you'll be able to learn the lesson of surrendering to your Buddha nature when it starts showing its bald head, and when things get really, really rough. Because they will.

This is a book about how travelling with Zen masters forces a particular kind of letting go. It's about the need to surrender everything we are, or think we are, if we are going to be serious about our spiritual growth. Not in the sense of permanent baldness (although that too could happen) but in this way: being bald needs to not matter in the same way that titles need to not matter, the size of our penises needs to not matter, and our income needs to not matter—assuming we can put a roof over our heads and food on our table. As long as they count, as long as we define ourselves by using the impermanent characteristics of our lives, we've created an invisible yet powerful barrier to spiritual growth—a 360-degree glass ceiling.

Before leaving for Korea, I had no first-hand experience of Korean zen. I had read stories, talked with visitors, and learned from Sunim. Those experiences felt secondhand somehow. I was hungry to know the monks. How gruff were they? Were they all like Sunim? Were monastic rules as strict as all the books implied? Even though I had been an ordained dharma teacher for years, and had spent three years in a Zen Buddhist seminary, I had never really been completely surrounded by Buddhism twenty-four hours a day. I had never been with a Zen master, a Sunim, let alone several, day in and day out. I had never been isolated from my life as a Western woman living out her days in the Midwest. Even in the temples in the United States there are National Public Radio newscasts, UPS deliveries, and quick trips to Whole Foods. It was easy to think of myself as a model Buddhist as long as I was surrounded by such comfort and exposure to my favorite attachments: news and trivial information, magazines, smoothies. Besides, a month was only thirty days. I could survive that on sheer will power if it came to that.

Chapter Two

Why Korea?

SOME KOREAN HISTORY
WITH BUDDHIST DATES MIXED IN

4000 B.C. (6,000 yrs. ago)	Human settlement discovered on the Korean peninsula as near as archeologists can tell.
2333 B.C.	The first kingdom of Ko-choson arose, founded by the legendary Tangun.
300 A.D.	The Kingdom of Koguryo is formed as the first independent Korean state. Koguryo is joined by the sister kingdom of Paekche.
400	The Silla dynasty surfaces.
527	Buddhism emerges as a state-supported religion.
617–686	Wonhyo does for Buddhism what Elvis did for rock 'n' roll.
632-647	Zen Buddhism appears.
676-935	Unification! The first three-dimensional Pac Man game results in Silla swallowing up the other two kingdoms.
742–935	The monarchies are pretty unstable and lots of juicy scandals abound.
935–1392	The Koryo dynasty. Country is basically being run by warrior aristocrats. Buddhism becomes the state religion for a while, leaving an indelible influence on the rest of Korea's history. Confucianism also greatly influ-

ences the country and its people during this period of economic prosperity. However, an inordinate amount of energy is expended fighting off the invading Chinese.

1122–1258   Civil disturbances start.

1172-1202   The peasant and slave liberation movement sweeps the country.

1231   The Mongols invade! The country is laid to waste for the next 25 years. They keep reappearing any time they are bored and want some wine, women, artifacts, and land. They keep up their pillaging until 1368. This alone explains why so many monasteries are way up in the mountains and why all the nuns have dogs.

1392-1910   This is the period of Choson, the last dynasty. The general who became the king threw the Buddhists out and confiscated monasteries right and left. Back up into the mountains went the monks and nuns.

1446   King Sejong pulls a group of scholars together and tells them he needs a user-friendly language. They develop Han-gul, which is comprised of only 10 vowels and 14 consonants. (If there was an Emmy award for languages, Han-gul would get it.)

1592   Japan's invasion of Korea that the Koreans *still* talk about. Basically the entire peninsula was rampaged and overrun in a month. The worst part was that the Japanese kidnapped anyone they thought had useful skills—from potters to managers to tradespeople. The Chinese finally came and helped the Koreans to eventually force the Japanese out.

1784   Christianity first appears. It spread like a computer virus for the next two centuries, representing modernization, Westernization, salvation, and offering a much easier spiritual path than Buddhism.

1870   French and American warships show up.

1882	The Chinese invade again.
1894	The Sino-Japanese War breaks out. Meanwhile the entire class system begins to break down. The Koreans only manage to avoid a civil war because they are too busy fighting all the outsiders who keep trying to invade the peninsula.
1910–1945	The thirty-five-year Japanese colonial rule is a miserable time for most Koreans.
1945	The establishment of the Republic of Korea.
1948	Korea is divided into two countries: the Republic of Korea (South Korea) and the Democratic People's Republic of Korea (North Korea).
1950–1953	The Korean War: North vs. South.
1972	The first whispered conversations about the possibility of reunification begin, at least in local tearooms.
1988	The 24th Olympiad in Seoul puts Korea on the worldwide television landscape.
1991	Both North and South Korea are admitted to the United Nations.
1992	Free elections are held in South Korea.

August 29, 1999, Heinsa

In the earliest days of the Choson dynasty, during the fourteenth century, followers of the Buddha couldn't go to the temples by royal decree. In those days, men tended to follow the Confucian way while women followed the Buddhist path in secret, except for one period when the queen ruled the country until her son was old enough to be ruler. She did her best to revitalize Buddhism in spite of the Confucians fighting her every effort. She gave secret orders to provide rice to the temples where the monks were starving to death and made a monk her personal advisor. When she stepped down from the throne to make way for her son, her monk advisor was banished to an island and killed. Sunim says that whenever women were influential Buddhism did better. I bet that's still true.

Riding on this bus feels like I'm riding in a time capsule backwards. Right now we're in about 1300 A.D.—teeny clay-roofed villages surrounded by rice fields and circled by mountains. No cars in sight. It's not like me to wax poetic on an empty stomach but it really does feel like we've driven right through a photograph and here we are part of the picture. Raining still. Pouring actually.

That the pilgrimage was in Korea mattered. It mattered because I wanted to live the stories instead of just hearing about them. We chant Korean chants in our temple. I wanted to understand why they all sound like love songs. Korea mattered because my teacher is Korean and I wanted to know if he was truly representative of Korean Zen masters or just some wild-eyed, wacky guy that I had the karmic fortune to literally stumble across.

Korea mattered because the Zen stories from Korea are so full of warrior effort and poignancy they make me cry, and I wanted to know why. Books about the country describe its sheer beauty and the height of its mountains. How had Buddhism survived in such a place, especially without cell phones? How did the people eat? How could they tell when spiritual travellers or marauders were climbing the mountain paths to visit for a day or to stay for a lifetime?

I wanted to know why every single Korean Buddhist I have ever met (except one businessman in Chicago) looks at me hard when we are introduced and when they are told I am a monk, either grins or laughs out loud, and then tries to feed me rice dishes or Korean pancakes or spiced cabbage.

What is it about Korea that creates people who just showed up to help when we were digging out from 10 feet of sewage at the start-up of our Chicago temple? And then having little or no money, sent us more Buddhas than we'll ever need: life-size Buddhas; gold ones.

Korea mattered because its mountains—fondly called the Asian Alps—had protected countless monasteries from being completely destroyed during foreign invasions and internal raids. Koreans have been able to maintain a pure form of Buddhism, surviving in the hermitages perched high above the clouds at the end of mountain trails and in the hearts of the monks and nuns who continue the practices passed down from the ancients. Korea's history of being conquered again and again inspires the almost samurai feistiness of its Buddhist practitioners and explains why Western students have been rare. The country is the perfect backdrop for a pilgrimaging woman from the other side of the world with its stories of romance, tragedy, scandals, and abiding determination not to be the runt of Asia's litter.

* * *

Coming from a country where history is measured in just a couple of centuries, Korea at over four thousand years old seems ancient. It was first settled by Chinese immigrants, Manchurians actually, although not many of the Koreans I met travelling were interested in talking about it much. The first official "Korean" civilization is believed to have been founded by a celestial being who had a real hankering for life on earth. When he just couldn't stand it any more he grabbed three thousand of his best friends and talked them into coming down to our realm. They landed right on the top of one of Korea's highest mountains, Mt. Paektu, and began the human civilization, a story that has yet to have a clear ending.

On a map Korea looks like a wizened old appendix, jutting out of the Chinese continent. It's not really that big, about 630 miles long by about 140 miles wide, although it feels big if you are travelling on foot or by bus. It is so beautiful, the mountains are right out of a movie. They are almost too perfect the way a model's face is too perfect: just the right

11

amount of craggy with spectacular wildflowers, including elf orchids and wandering roses, and all sorts of flowering trees perfuming the trails. And at almost every turn along the mountain trails are rocky streams of rushing water and waterfalls, and panoramic views to break your heart.

By the time of Christ's birth, Korea had established a relationship with China—mostly of fighting off invasions and losing. Finally, in 313 A.D., the kingdom of Koguryo overthrew its Chinese warlord, becoming the first truly independent Korean state. In the Fourth Century A.D., Koguryo was joined by a sister kingdom, Paekche, and a century later the Silla dynasty rose to power in what is now South Korea. Greedy for territory, Silla tried to take over Paekche. A furious Paekche kingdom allied its forces with those of Koguryo. The Japanese complicated matters by becoming allied with Paekche which forced Silla to become an ally to its old enemy China. (Feel free to draw yourself a little diagram on the borders of the page to keep track of all this.) After years of some of the most brutal wars in the history of humankind, the Chinese-Silla alliance overwhelmed the two other kingdoms, finally creating a unified Korea.

Despite all of these culture clashes, Koreans have always had a deep thirst for spiritual solace. Even its flag demonstrates this historic yearning for harmony, balance, and both inner and outer peace: it consists of a red and blue circle on a sea of white, framed by a set of four trigrams. (The trigrams are like the ones in the *I Ching*.) The circle is divided into two equal parts with a wavy line through the middle. The upper half, the red half, represents the positive cosmic forces in our lives. The blue section represents the negative forces. When they dance together on a waving flag they represent the harmony that can come from a life lived wisely. The trigrams surrounding the circle represent the four universal elements that surround and nourish us as we move toward our own enlightenment: heaven, earth, fire, and water. It would make a great ankle tattoo.

Given their penchant for spirituality, their love of nature, and a sort of earthy wildness largely unknown to Westerners. Koreans were a natural match for Buddhism. Its teachings of living a life of balance in the form of equanimity and deep respect for the four elements were openly welcomed by the Korean people when it first spread from India, toward the end of the fourth century. Buddhism spread rapidly and was adopted as the official state religion of Silla in the early fifth century. Even in Paekche most of the kings and members of the upper classes became Buddhists. Temples began appearing high on the mountaintops where they would be safe from invaders and where some still remain.

The spread of Buddhism, particularly during the Silla reign, was in large part the result of the martyrdom of a prominent court official named Ich'adon. The story is that Ich'adon showed up at the king's palace one day and announced that he was a Buddhist. The king was livid and ordered that Ich'adon be beheaded. But when the executioner cut off Ich'adon's head there was no blood. Instead, milk flowed from the terrible wound. In the wake of this rather surreal miracle, many of the king's court immediately became followers of Buddhism. So many, in fact, that the king decided it would be a good idea to name Buddhism as the nation's "official" religion.

The remote, high mountains provided a natural shelter away from worldly concerns—one that fed the spontaneous, direct, and self-reliant style that characterizes Korean Zen. Wonhyo was a monk who lived in Korea in the seventh century and spent much of his time writing books— about 180 of them. He was so determined to find enlightenment that he decided to travel to China in search of a Zen master. But after drinking blood from a skull one night because he couldn't see it in the dark and thought it was a bowl of water (a disgusting but powerful experience of the senses), he decided he didn't really need a teacher after all. The experience showed him the mind's ability to create our reality. Wonhyo was a wild man's wild man. He taught Buddhism by way of skits and plays, a little flame throwing thrown in for visual effect. Wonhyo gave everyone permission to do their best to find their hearts, something the Korean people desperately needed.

During the fifth and sixth centuries, both Korea and Buddhism blossomed. Temples, many of them still standing, began appearing all over the country attracting serious students of the Buddhist teachings, mostly the Avatamsaka Sutra and the Lotus Sutra, two of the most robust teachings. Amitabha, the Buddha of Light, and Avalokitesvara, the Bodhisattva of Great Compassion, became national guardian angels. As the spark of Zen took hold, there was an increasing emphasis on meditation and direct experience as the most efficient path to enlightenment. Over time, nine different Zen schools emerged, known as the Nine Mountains of Son.

Korea's rough and tumble history wouldn't allow Buddhism to spread smoothly. In 935 A.D., Silla fell to the kingdom of Koryo, and things changed dramatically. A central bureaucracy was created, provinces were formally divided into prefectures, and military rule became the law of the land. A class system emerged where aristocratic families were served by commoners. Monks began fighting with each other over rituals and scripture and about how much actual practice a person needed to do to authentically achieve enlightenment. Happily a heroic monk named Chinul decided to make it his life's work to weave the various threads of Korean Buddhism together into one whole piece of cloth. Much to everyone's amazement he pulled it off by founding a temple, Songgwangsa, as a base camp for the merged schools. Songgwangsa was the command central of Korean Buddhism for the next three hundred years. Finally, in the fourteenth century, the monk T'aego (1301–1382) formally unified all of the various Zen sects under the name Chogye.

All during this period, various Chinese marauders kept invading Korea. The worst were the Mongols who invaded the country six times in twenty-five years during the 1200s. Although the Koreans were able to eventually fight them off, the Mongols still managed to capture some 206,000 men and women to take home as slaves, an act some Koreans have yet to forgive.

The worst of the invaders were known as the Red Turbans; they dominated the country through the fourteenth century while Japanese pirates rampaged the southern and western coasts. These constant invasions led to the eventual fall of the Kingdom of Koryo. In 1392 Confucian society emerged out of the rubble. Korea renamed itself Choson, or Land of the Morning Calm, and the brand new capital city of Seoul was built. A series of monarchs worked hard to redesign the government structure, rebuild a military force, and promote economic growth.

Happily their efforts worked. Korea grew and prospered. Society evolved into a formal class system where extended families were the glue that kept communities together and men were definitely the authority figures. The way one moved up the social ladder was to work for the government and the way to work for the government was to pass excruciatingly difficult civil service exams that make our contemporary exams pale in comparison, except for maybe law boards. Following the development of its amazingly simple yet brilliant language, Han-gul, in the fifteenth century, Koreans spent the next few hundred years making names for themselves in the areas of science, technology, art, and architecture.

But the calm of the fifteenth century didn't last. Determined to be master of the world, the Emperor of Japan sent 160,000 troops to conquer Korea once and for all in 1592. After five years, when the Koreans still hadn't capitulated, another 140,000 Japanese troops arrived. This time they almost succeeded. What saved Korea was the construction of the world's first armored warship, affectionately called the Turtle Ship. In pictures these boats really do look like wooden turtles, head and all, with eight long flippers coming out from each side. Enabling the Koreans to defeat the Japanese troops at sea, the Turtle Ship changed the course of the war.

After the Japanese were finally run off, the Korean peninsula was once again in a shambles. Right about then the first European appeared in the form of Jan Janse Weltevree (1627), a trader who found himself shipwrecked on the Korean shore. The next hundred years brought more Europeans, major political reforms including a move toward real democracy, and the usual invasions from Japan and Manchuria. In the 1870s, France and the United States entered the mix in response to the execution of a handful of French priests in 1866 and the sinking of an American ship, the General Sherman. If that wasn't bad enough for Koreans, who were definitely experiencing a major case of invader fatigue, a German self-styled political advisor by the name of Ernest Oppert appeared on the scene only to spend the rest of his life robbing tombs and providing not so great advice to Korean political leaders about how to deal with newly influential Western powers.

Not to be outmaneuvered by other outsiders, the Japanese showed up again in 1875, forcing the Korean government, under threat of yet another war, to sign a treaty with Japan to "establish diplomatic and commercial relations." In the meantime, Korean scholars and government officials began to visit other countries, bringing back innovations ranging from the concept of a modern farm to a postal service system. These modern concepts and institutions looked so enticing to the Chinese that they just couldn't leave Korea vulnerable to the Japanese, so they also attacked the country yet again, overthrowing the government in 1882.

By the end of the nineteenth century the Koreans had had it. They were sick to death of all the foreign invasions and furious with the growing corruption of the government. A revolution began. At the same moment, China and Japan decided to have a shoot-out to see who was going to take over Korea next. Japan won round one only to be pushed out a year later by Russian, German, and French military patrols. Convinced that someone would kill him for little or no reason, the king fled to Russia. By 1896, the two countries still wrestling for control over Korea were Russia and Japan. Japan finally won.

Exhausted and frustrated by continual invasions, the Korean people began to formally call for major political reform and, ultimately, independence. Buddhism, which had taken refuge in the mountains, began to take on a larger role in the lives of individual spiritual seekers. Local newspapers started calling for not only independence but enlightenment of the people. By 1919 a national independence movement had formed and a Declaration of Independence was written. Two million people rallied behind it. The Japanese military regime responded by burning down thousands of homes and churches and arresting more than 26,700 Koreans. Another 2,000 were wounded or killed. Some of the leaders of the move for independence fled to Shanghai to set up a provisional government while others went to the United States.

As soon as World War II started the provisional government of Korea declared war on Japan. Let's just say that things went downhill from there. Groups expressing even the slightest anti-Japanese sentiment were ordered to disband and people began to disappear. Japan declared that the Japanese language would be Korea's national language and attendance at Shinto shrine ceremonies was made mandatory. Names had to be changed to Japanese ones and military service was compulsory.

Ironically, the strain of Buddhism the Japanese brought with them during their most recent invasion of Korea (T'aego) proved to be troublesome to Korean Buddhists. The Japanese occupation demanded that monks marry. The ones who didn't disappeared. The result was a schism among Korean monks that is only now beginning to heal in any significant way. According to the history books and tourist guides, there are now eighteen Buddhist sects on the peninsula, but they are hard to spot. The Chogye order seems to be dominant despite repeated news stories of internal fights for political control. A feisty order grounded in realism, Chogye promises to be the key player in driving Buddhism's unfolding through the twenty-first century.

Only with the end of the Second World War did Japanese colonial rule in Korea finally end. No sooner had the Japanese packed up and left than the Soviet Union moved in. American troops soon followed suit, splitting the country in half—north and south. Today the split continues with political tensions periodically bubbling to the surface. Rumor has it the split won't last much longer. South Korea, where we travelled, is a democracy, having been formally created as the Republic of South Korea in 1948, with Seoul as its capital. The country continues to experience a massive transformation from an agrarian economy to a manufacturing and service economy. Illiteracy is virtually nonexistent, the mass media is everywhere, and teenagers look like they've stepped right out of an MTV music video. Reunification with North Korea is a national obsession and a vision of a strong peaceful nation, free of marauders, is embedded in the hearts of Koreans.

ITEMS PACKED FOR THE PILGRIMAGE

2 sets of heavy cotton Gray Robes

2 pairs of Victoria's Secret gray cotton bikini underpants (what was I thinking?!)

2 Victoria's Secret gray cotton bras (with no underwire for maximum comfort)

2 brand new white Fruit of the Loom cotton tee shirts for men, medium

2 pairs of brand new all white cotton socks from Target

1 fist-sized copy of the Dhammapada

1 fist-sized copy of the Diamond Sutra

8 Nature Valley granola bars

4 Think Bars—sort of like granola bars only more solid, more fruity, and more crammed full of vitamins and minerals

1 green army surplus store flashlight, including a plastic red cover to put over the light

1 bottle of 25 Tylenol tablets—I figured I wouldn't need one every day

1 tube of Close Up toothpaste

1 small inexpensive camera (to accommodate my penchant for losing cameras in unmindful moments)

1 aerosol can of Off

1 tube of Benadryl

1 Meijer's brand cinnamon-flavored dental floss

2 pairs of glasses, both old, both unfashionable

1 bottle of Women's Health Care Complex multivitamins

1 travelling kite, neon pink, in a pouch—lent to me by Carolyn Christopher, true friend

1 plastic card, "International Translator," with pictures of taxis, doctors, toilets, food, etc.—also from Carolyn

1 time converter card—you guessed it: from Carolyn

2 AA batteries

1 gray cotton hat, sort of like the ones you see in the L.L. Bean catalogue only I got it in a surf shop in Hawaii

4 pens

1 Mennen's for Men deodorant stick

1 Swiss Army knife from Allen Moy who is always thinking about my physical safety. Too bad he keeps moving far away...

1 bag of Hall's lemon honey drops

2 lined composition books, both blank, except for motivational quotes glued to their covers

1 pack of water purification tablets

1 bag of Kool Aid Lemonade mix for the purified water

1 packet of Pepcid tablets

2 earplugs

1 wrist rosary

10 tampons (lasted all of a day. Don't worry, I won't talk about it after this. Let's just say that part of why I ended up with no socks and one borrowed tee shirt by the trip's end was related to only having 10 tampons. Enough said.)

1 pair of brand new hiking boots

1 water bottle

10 packs of Winterfresh gum

THE ITINERARY AS BEST I REMEMBER *

August 22, 1999	Chicago, Illinois
August 23	Seoul, Korea The House of Sharing
August 28	Taegu
August 29	Heinsa Temple
August 31	Taegu Sokkuram Grotto
September 1	Pulguksa Temple Kyongju
September 2	Popchangsa Temple
September 3	Tongdosa Temple
September 5	Pomosa Temple Pusan
September 6	Naewonsa Temple Ssanggesa Temple
September 7	Chilbulsa Temple
September 8	Yongwonsa Temple Sonwonju Hermitage
September 9	Shilsangsa Temple Hwaomsa Temple
September 10	Songgwangsa Temple
September 12	Naesosa Temple
September 14	Taegu
September 15	Unmunsa Temple and Nuns' College
September 18	Yosu
September 20	Seoul
September 20 again	Chicago, Illinois

* The only "itinerary" we had was in Sunim's mind. He usually told us the
names and stories of the places we were about to visit or had just visited

during daily 4 A.M. lectures in his room. To tell the truth, sometimes I was just too tired to hear what he was saying let alone write it down. Plus, the trip changed moment by moment which meant that we might start out for one place and end up at another place entirely by the end of the day.

Chapter Three

On Korean Soil:
A Juicy Beginning

Journal entry: August 23, 1999, Seoul

"Arrived! 6,515 miles in a day thanks to the wonders of modern aviation. Within the first five minutes of our flight we were travelling 268 miles per hour. Korean soap operas on the plane. Homesick already. Practice strong. This will be a great pilgrimage. The Diamond Sutra makes more sense by the minute. Seoul is huge. River framed. Bright colors are everywhere. It's as though Crayola let loose on everything. Cars are bright purple, green. Rainbows are painted on posts and walls. Everyone has his own cellular phone. Most people seem to be using them, each with its own song to announce a new caller. Even the roofs on the houses look like bright clay tubing. I can't believe how calm I feel, how eager. Ready for anything."

This story really begins five years ago when I had one of those heart-thumping, nausea-filled, dizzy-as-you-sink-to-the-ground panic attacks. It happened when I was sitting in the dermatology clinic at the University of Michigan Hospital with my daughter. She had a mole her doctor thought might be cancerous. Ever in complete control of my emotions, things seemed to be okay until I sat down in the waiting room with her. Suddenly I remembered sitting in a chair for a mole of my own—a tiny dot on an eyelid—two years earlier. It had been cancerous and I had gone through a serious surgery to get it and its growing tentacles out of my face. Here was my baby possibly facing a similar fate.

When I started to slip I remember mumbling that I'd wait out in the corridor, wobbled my way to the door, and in an effort to not fall face down on the floor, gracefully slid myself down a wall until I was lying down next to it.

In less than a minute, two nurses were kneeling next to me helping me up and walking me into one of the clinic's examination rooms, my daughter in gentle tow. There a team of doctors looked at her mole, pronounced it cancer free and casually mentioned over their shoulders that there was no reason to live with anxiety in this day and age. Lots of medications were available to take the edge off of any emotionally painful situations. "No thanks, " I said. I'll go it alone.

Even though I never had another panic attack, I've spent all the years since then practicing panic prevention; looking ahead to what might go wrong; planning for ways to deal with unforeseeable events that could become emotionally difficult. Shaving my head is a perfect example of the delusion of control. Knowing that I would have to shave my head, because it was one of the nonnegotiables of the pilgrimage, I did my all-time best to control the experience to lessen the shock. Bobbing my shoulder-length hair seemed okay. Then after performing a wedding ceremony the weekend before leaving for Korea, I asked my friend Joy Naylor to cut off all the hair that could be cut with scissors. Even that was mostly okay. I could pull a baseball cap over my head and pretend that I was trying to look like Demi Moore in *G.I. Jane*.

Next, my dharma brother Joe Lukomski came at my scalp with an electric razor. It took about an hour. Although there were a couple flashes of nausea and my heart did ramp up a bit, there was no panic attack. Surely this was proof enough that I was definitely over any emotional hump I needed to get past. Surely nothing could be harder than watching the last of my hair hit the ground unless it was the discovery of a huge red birthmark on the left side of the back of my head shaped like a big fat deformed insect from another universe. Or maybe a river rat. I named it Ben.

And then... Looking in the mirror for the first time, hair free, the palpitations started. I was losing me. The bald person staring back didn't even look like me, didn't look female, didn't look Western, didn't look Irish. It was just this blank face with two eyes, a nose, and a mouth that any third grader could draw given half a chance. I chanted until my heart slowed down and my palms stopped sweating, congratulating myself for being so Buddhalike in what would surely be the most difficult part of the trip. Since my heart didn't even react when I was instructed by Sunim to get my head shaved again the next day I was certain that all of the bad hair days of my life were over. No more raw emotional moments for this Bodhisattva! I was Xena the Warrior Princess and nothing was going to get in the path of this woman on a mission to liberate all beings in one lifetime.

✳ ✳ ✳

The Buddha's first words in the Dhammapada are:
"We are what we think.
All that we are arises with our thoughts.
With our thoughts we make the world."

(*Dhammapada: The Sayings of the Buddha,*
A Rendering by Thomas Byrom. Shambala, Boston, 1993, p.1)

After twelve years of determined practice I am convinced Buddha is right and that the first time a person actually sees this in himself or herself is the first genuine taste of enlightenment. Prior to Korea, the few times I had somehow managed to simply be in a situation without sailing off into a sea of opinions were wonderful. Without any thinking about it, I somehow knew exactly what to do, what the wisdom of the moment was. It almost felt channeled. Sometimes I would find myself saying things or doing things that were a surprise even to me. Like yelling at a huge man to back off when he was about to grab a teenager who had given him the finger. We were both so surprised we ended up laughing together while the kid ran away, hopefully keeping his finger to himself for all time. Or once, selling a woman a book, I saw such sadness in her eyes that I just took her in my arms while she sobbed. It was her first Christmas in over twenty years without her husband. Or stopping short on a walk in the woods near home, entranced by wild miniature pansies.

There was a sweet spaciousness in those moments—combined with this crazy feeling of being in love with everything—the man, the kid, the woman, the pansies. Getting onto the plane in Chicago I wanted more of these timeless moments. It seemed like a pilgrimage would provide the perfect foil for sharpening the mindfulness that somehow lead into that sweet state.

Packing for the trip in Ann Arbor, I resolved to stay in "don't know" mind for the entire pilgrimage. I would just be with whatever happened. No anger. No neediness. No sadness. No crazed excitement. Instead I would spend thirty days as a female Thich Nhat Hanh, offering Korea "peace in every step."

That I was beside myself with excitement making the resolve should have been the first clue that there might be some rocky roads ahead. Some part of me whispered that I was going into this pilgrimage with about a mountain's worth too much ego; that I was emphasizing goals, assuming conditions, prejudging outcomes; that part of me, the whispering part, said, "Slow down, be humble, just let the thinking stop. Don't force anything. Just let go, P'arang. Just keep your heart soft."

But I didn't listen.

The four of us travelling together, Samu Sunim, Haju, Kaeo (more on Kaeo in a minute), and I are all well-trained (from our Western perspective anyway) longstanding Buddhists. All of us are ordained. Samu Sunim

had made pilgrimages through the mountains at least a dozen times during his thirty years on North American soil. Haju Sunim had been a student of Sunim's since the 1980s and knew him well. She had also been
to Korea before—on a pilgrimage that lasted several months. She already
knew some of the people and places we would be visiting. I figured she
would coach me through the unclear parts.

Kaeo Sunim, a young Korean monk, in his twenties by my guess, had
just arrived in the United States to serve Sunim as his personal attendant.
With family in Korea, Kaeo had been to many of the temples—large and
small—and seemed strong enough to carry the rest of us and all our bag-
gage too. I had already spent two five-day retreats with Kaeo, leading one
of them. I knew him to be smart, quick, and knowledgeable about Korean
Buddhist customs and monastery protocol. Kaeo also has a wonderful
childlike sense of humor that I was sure we would need at some point
since we were mostly travelling on uncharted territory as the first Western female monks visiting some of the mountain hermitages.

And then there was me: Bald. Excited. Apprehensive because there
was no set itinerary. Keeping a third eye out for palpitations. Willing to
try my hand at just trusting and staying open. I was going for Eagle Scout
status in Dharma land.

Because I had promised to perform a wedding ceremony for close
friends on the day before we were supposed to leave the States, Haju and
I drove into the night to get back to Chicago in time to catch the plane.
Upon arriving at the Chicago temple to catch up with Sunim and Kaeo,
we slammed into a world of barked orders. "You have too much luggage!
Fit everything into one small backpack, a small cloth one, or leave it
behind!"

By the time the four of us got on the plane I had given up my suit-
case, as well as half of the things packed in it—the 25 Tylenol pills, the
extra Victoria's Secret gray cotton bikini underpants that perfectly
matched our robes, the brand new lightweight earth-toned almost-

without-leather hiking boots. The deodorant for the plane ride home, the guidebook of Korea. Now packed into a monk's gray sack were two sets of robes, earplugs, a toothbrush, toothpaste, glasses, antibiotic cream, my passport, an International Translator, and, I admit it, my Working Assets VISA card. Oh yeah, and a half-inch metal Buddha, a gift from my dharma brother Sam Clark, to hold in the palm of my hand in case the going got rough (which I completely forgot I had, so a lot of good it did me).

As soon as we settled into our seats, Haju told me that we would have to tie the wide-bottomed pants we wore under our robes around our ankles in a particular way each day. To keep them in place we would need special "cuffs" which she would show me how to make. So we spent a good chunk of the flight hand-stitching long gray cotton laces to tie around our ankles over our pants and socks. The laces never did work. During the whole pilgrimage every time we stopped my first move was to bend from the waist to the ground where I would try to quickly retie the laces so they would stop coming undone. It didn't matter. They untied themselves, the pants freed themselves, and I was constantly in trouble. On days when I couldn't find the laces during the 3 A.M. wake-ups, I would desperately try to cram the pant legs into my socks. That never worked either.

The in-flight soap opera gave us a taste of Korean life experience as we flew over the Pacific. In the French movies I grew up with if there wasn't heartbreak, desperation, and tragedy then it wasn't considered romance. Korean filmmakers must have been raised on the same films. Sacrificing self for the greater good was the constant theme in the movie. I wondered how much the theme would play out on the pilgrimage. Would we all end up taking turns letting go of what we wanted to do, where we wanted to visit? Would I even get a vote? Would the Korean Zen masters accept Haju and me as monks? Would they treat her as Sunim's dharma heir for the sake of introducing Buddhism to more Westerners, or would we face a brick wall of ancient rules and hierarchies? What would be the pilgrimage's unexpected ending?

A hurricane of thoughts kept me awake for the whole flight. While everyone else slept I conjured up scenarios of how the trip might play out given what I knew of Kaeo, Sunim, and Haju, adding the movie's theme of giving up one's own happiness for the sake of others, for the greater good.

Landing in Seoul on August 23 (4 A.M. Ann Arbor time), we headed straight for the mountains just outside the city to the House of Sharing, which turned out to be home to a handful of elderly Korean women and the young monk who cares for them. Right then and there I completely lost all resolve to stay in "don't know" mind, to simply be with whatever was going on. Nothing in my life prepared me for the intensity of the House of Sharing. Getting out of the car from the airport I glanced up at a two-story dormitory surrounded by fields on two sides with a road and a hill on the other. Circling to look around I could only gasp. About four feet away from us was a large sculpture, maybe ten feet high, of a naked woman who had sunk into the ground up to her waste. She was aqua colored and clearly in agony. Her body, thin arms, and sagging breasts looked worn, her face, exhausted. Beside the statue a second building housed historical documents and tape recordings.

We had driven into a living museum—a housing compound for women who had been the sex slaves of Japanese soldiers during World War II. The Japanese military kidnapped thousands, some say as many as 300,000, girls and women for the purpose of satisfying the soldiers' sexual proclivities. Girls as young as eleven were taken from their families. Most were sent directly to military bases where they serviced as many as thirty men each day.

After we had taken our backpacks into the small bedrooms where we would spend our first night in Korea, the young resident monk escorted us into the small brick depository of documents. There we saw huge photographs of long lines of Japanese soldiers waiting to go through a door of what looked like a plain house. Behind it were the comfort women. Each soldier was allowed to have sex with one woman one time until his next sex appointment. That way the line would keep moving so each woman could serve her quota of soldiers for the day. Usually the number was between twenty-five and thirty soldiers. Officers had it even better. They could choose their sex partner and were permitted to stay overnight with the women so they wouldn't have to rush or limit themselves to only one sex act.

In Okinawa alone there were 130 "comfort stations."

The experience either cost the women their lives or drove them to insanity. The women who are still alive have not only survived, but are determined to hold the Japanese government accountable for the sex crimes committed against them. That's where we stayed, with seven women, now in their eighties, who somehow survived such a brutal experience. This unexpected encounter became a giant test of resolve. Expect anything? Enjoy it all? How could I listen to the audiotaped stories of what each woman went through and not hate the Japanese soldiers?

I watched Sunim's face closely as we talked with the women long into the night. I had never witnessed him in such an intense situation— one filled with such heartbreak and rage. While his face never changed expression I could feel his energy shift. Was it compassion? Anger? I wanted to run outside, get back on a plane, and go home. I didn't know how I would feel the next time I looked into the eyes of a Japanese man of authority—even a monk. Did he know about the comfort women? Was he capable of the same behavior? Would any of us ever be free from the consequences of such brutality?

Only days before I had heard a similar story coming out of Tibet— only this time it was Chinese soldiers attacking Buddhist nuns. But it hadn't happened fifty years ago—it happened in the 1990s. Instead of sex with lines of soldiers, the nuns were shocked with cattle prods on their genitals. The nuns committed suicide to end the torture. The comfort women I was with told us that they had decided to do whatever they had to do to live. Their stories broke my heart and I honestly thought I had heard everything anyone had to say, having worked with domestic violence shelters for some twenty plus years.

When the Korean women first came forward to authorities with their stories about ten years ago, nobody believed them. The Japanese government accused them of lying. Then someone anonymously made Japanese government documents public, proving the truth of the women's words. As of this writing, there still hasn't been an official response from the Japanese government acknowledging the crimes (informally Japanese officials have said that they needed "comfort stations" to prevent the soldiers from simply raping all the women in liberated areas, to limit the spread of venereal disease, and to "smooth out local opposition"). The women pile into a bus every Wednesday morning and go to Seoul to protest in front of the Japanese embassy, these seven tiny ancient women and one young monk. When they aren't protesting, they're gardening and painting and working at the small museum adding to the documentation. Early on in our visit I asked one of the women why they don't try to forget what happened. She answered, "We have a duty to leave our story." So they retell and retell and retell.

Staying at the House of Sharing, I wanted to wallow in my fury at the soldiers' treatment of the women, so many of them just young girls when they were seized, younger than my daughter. I just couldn't believe that the Japanese government would simply refuse to admit to any wrongdoing. It was like our pretending that the United States doesn't have a huge gaping wound called racism that we need to heal. It was like our pretending that the heartbreak of slavery and indentured servitude is past tense. It isn't.

I lay awake that night obsessing about how I could help the women. I decided that my resolution to simply be with a situation didn't make sense.

I kept trying to reconcile Buddha's teaching that we create our problems with our minds with what I was experiencing. If the women don't protest, if they don't hold on to their fury, how would anything change? And if we don't join them in their outrage, when will the horrors end? Over and over the same question kept circling in my mind: "What is the middle way here? Where's the wisdom?" I half expected Sunim to announce that we would spend the entire pilgrimage helping the women with their documentary paperwork.

The next morning—our first in Korea—we woke up early. I think it was 3 A.M. The women had prepared an enormous breakfast for us of rice, Korean pancakes, and a feast of various vegetable dishes. Sunim announced that we would first have a formal meditation service together—the four of us and the comfort women—in their small meditation hall. We climbed the narrow outside stairs of one of the buildings to a room that was a cross between an art gallery and a cathedral. Along one wall was a collection of huge paintings created by several of the women as a form of art therapy. Some of the paintings were dark and heavy with spiky forms and clouds. Others were surprisingly light and filled with flowers and figures of young beautiful women. Across the room from the paintings was a wall of tiny lit candles and an altar.

We did prostrations. We chanted. We sat in meditation. Then Sunim, who was facing the rest of us, raised his eyes. He quietly looked at each woman. Then, in almost a whisper, he said, "They treated you so badly. They took away your youth and innocence." A pause. "Look at the young monk giving you his youth and life." A silence. "If you don't forgive your captors you'll be the same as them. If you forgive them, they'll feel ashamed. If they don't get it, future generations will. For your own sake you should forgive them... You have become resentful... I would hope that you don't die resentful. For your own sake so you'll die happier."

I couldn't believe it! He was asking them, pleading with them, to give up everything they were clinging to. Everything. Wasn't there a warrior

Zen tradition that would give them permission to try to kick some very deserving Japanese butt?!

The women listened. Several had bowed heads. Two looked Sunim straight in the eye as he talked. One argued back. He held his ground. They had to forgive. We have to forgive. All of us. Everything.

After a while the feeling in the room shifted. It became lighter, more hopeful, happier. I could literally feel the power of Buddha's words, "With your mind you make the world." Sunim was asking them to make a different world, a world of forgiveness. In that world they would create the possibility of a peaceful future for the generations lining up behind us. The women nodded slightly. They would still protest. But with a different purpose—to remind the world of what can and does happen when we don't take care of each other, when we don't protect each other, and when we don't speak up. We ate breakfast with the women, hearts light, giggling and hugging.

* * *

Almost from the moment we arrived at the House of Sharing I hit it off with one of the women. We started holding each other's hands when we met and didn't stop until I climbed in the car to leave. Her story was typical. She spent seven years in one room in a camp in Africa servicing as many as two dozen soldiers a day, sometimes more. Occasionally she was taken to a boat to spend up to three months on board taking care of the sailors. All of the other comfort women who were in Africa with her are now dead. She will be soon. When it was time for me to say good-bye to her she started to cry and clung to me. "You are my lost daughter! You are my lost daughter!" I was the baby the soldiers had taken from her at birth, returned at last, and as a monk no less. It was as though her life had come full circle. And instead of bitterness her gift to the world was me. She stood with tears in her eyes as we climbed into the car, and waved at me for as long as she could see us. I could only cry, not willing or able to imagine her heartbreak at the loss of her baby. Barely able to take in the raw love that was in her smile as she stood there waving. And you know, I *was* her daughter. I was the daughter of each and every one of those women. We all are.

That woman gave me courage. My panic attacks stopped. Given all she had lived through, her concern was only for my well being. She didn't want anything for herself. I wanted to give her back a kinder, saner world, one where atrocities couldn't happen. As a first step, I would offer up whatever the trip asked of me. And I would see it through. For her. And for those Japanese soldiers.

Chapter Four

The Pattern
of Our Days

Journal entry: September 12, 1999, Naesosa

"Here's the pattern: At three or four in the morning, depending on whether we are in the city or the country, we hear the *moktak*. A quick rush to the bathroom, fold up our bedding, no need to get dressed since we already are. Quickly walk to the meditation hall. Figure out where the heck we're supposed to stand—it's different in each place. One hundred and eight prostrations. Then, dripping in sweat, we chant *Yebul*, always beautiful, and the Heart Sutra, always confusing.

On to Sunim's room. One prostration followed by a lecture. Then breakfast: rice, soup, six side dishes (spicy vegetables), and, if we're lucky, some form of protein, maybe tofu, and sometimes little black beans. Then to the bathroom to rinse our faces and hands, brush our teeth, and we're off! Sometimes we visit a monk and Haju, Kaeo, and I sit for one to two hours (arg!) while he and Sunim chat in Korean. Our bottoms on hard floors. No cushions. In half lotus. I'm usually trying not to grimace within the first forty-five minutes. Keeping my back straight. Only flashes of concentration make it through the muscle spasms that come from not moving. Usually we are offered green tea, occasionally coffee. The nuns always give us pine needle tea. Yesterday it was definitely alcoholic—I could feel the buzz. Made it easier to climb though. Grin."

After the House of Sharing it was an emotional relief to return to downtown Seoul to stay in a Buddhist temple with monks. In the city monastic days begin at 4 A.M. with the sound of bells, gongs, and a big carved wooden fish. In the country drums add to the "Good morning Korea!" sound. Whatever the instrument, they are whacked hard so that all sentient beings within hearing distance know it's time to start the day. Each of the sounds is aimed at a particular audience. The drum's job is to wake up animals. Large bells call to anyone who has "become decadent" or given in to his or her own version of anger, greed, and/or delusion. I noticed the bell sounds the most. The wooden fish call to all who live in water and the gongs call to beings who live in the air. No one is left out.

There is a wonderful Zen teaching that summarizes another role for the different sounds: One day the seventeenth patriarch was walking with one of his students. Suddenly he turned to the young man. "What is ringing, the wind or the bells?" The student replied, "The wind is not ringing, the bells are not ringing, the mind is ringing." The Zen master looked at the student: "This is really true. What is ringing, the wind or the bells, or both? Whatever we say it doesn't hit the mark. So finally we find a solution, that the mind is ringing. This is very true, but still there is a question. What is the mind?" To this question the disciple replied, "Tranquility, imperturbability." The seventeenth ancestor was really pleased with this answer.

Dainin Katagiri, a much beloved Zen master of the twentieth century, offers an additional, deeper explanation of the meaning of the sounds of the bell and fish: According to Katagiri, Dogen Zenji, one of Buddhism's best known teachers, used to say: "'It is the wind ringing, it is the chimes ringing, it is the blowing ringing, it is the ringing ringing.' Ringing ringing means that ringing entrusts itself to ringing, settles into ringing, and manifests itself in creative activity. At that moment ringing is all—pervading without having any obstruction." (*Returning to Silence:*

Zen Practice in Daily Life by Dainin Katagiri. Shambala, Boston and London, 1988, p. 101)

Here is awakeness. No mind making the world.

Hmmmmm... Bells? Fish? Gongs? Drums? Forget drumming drumming when you are crawling around on your hands and knees in the dark in a completely foreign room, trying to remember where you put your glasses just before you fell asleep four hours ago (assuming you got that much sleep). Trying-not-to-squish-ants practice or don't-disturb-anyone-else practice takes precedence over any enlightenment experience. Especially when your under-the-breath curse that happens when you crawl over your glasses can be heard two rooms away. "Just this" I kept whispering to myself. Keep "Don't know" mind. It was worth a try. At least after the House of Sharing I had the motivation.

By the second day in Seoul I figured out that daily life in the monasteries really serves two purposes. First, it provides refuge in that each day's schedule is incredibly structured—down to the minute. As a result there is no need (or opportunity) to plan or wonder what your day will be like. The pattern has been set for a thousand years. So a sense of safety exists now that marauders have pretty much stopped burning down temples. The second purpose is to suck your ego right out of your system. This is accomplished through a combination of minutely detailed rules of protocol, a total ignoring of anything related to personal beauty or attractiveness (many of the bathrooms and all of the monks' rooms we were in were mirror free), and for this eight-hours-of-sleep-a-night-should-just-about-do-it Westerner, inhumane limits on sleep time. As an added bonus, there is a total lack of furniture—no chairs, no beds, no couches—unless you are lucky enough to be meeting with an abbot. So intense physical discomfort gets added to the ego-deleting tool kit.

Wherever we went, I never knew where to stand. For the entire pilgrimage I mostly stood in exactly the wrong place, unknowingly breaking some rule in some rule book. Usually the monks just ignored me. Sometimes one would motion me to stand behind a particular cushion if we happened to be in a meditation hall. It wasn't until the end of the trip that I understood that there is a strict pecking order for where people stand in just about every monastic situation, where people sit when they eat, and how they walk. In the meditation halls especially, the young acolyte monks stand right at the front of the hall, close to the altar, with senior monks standing farther toward the back. It's probably a good thing that I never knew the protocol. I would have reached a new level of paranoia about screwing up, probably making me so nuts you would still find me standing in some Korean meditation hall today, correcting my appropriate standing distance from the altar inch by painful inch. I stood in so many abbot's spots I can't believe they let me stay. One monk, after a number of obviously ignorant moves on my part, calmly walked me to the front of the room where I was so close to the Buddha figure on the altar I could have wiped his nose. I'm guessing he was trying to help me focus on what matters—meditation practice—instead of the rules of place and position. Or maybe he was getting such a kick out of my mistakes he didn't want to miss anything. Hard to say. At another temple a monk directed me to a spot beside the altar, way in front of the rest of those attending the service. It's a miracle nobody laughed out loud at my mistakes now that I think about it. Really well trained, those monks and nuns.

* * *

In every temple following the early morning gong, fish, and drum serenades, morning services formally start with the gonging of a huge bell, typically the size of a grown man. A big man. It gongs twenty-eight times. Then a monk with a *moktak* (a handheld carved wooden fish) guides those in the meditation hall through a formal service consisting of chanting and prostrations. At each temple, Haju and I did the most prostrations: every morning, at least 108. Sometimes more. When everyone else stopped we kept going unless Sunim told us to stop. Sometimes we would still be doing prostrations after all the young monks or nuns had left the meditation hall. I was glad to do them, figuring that the sight of two middle-aged Western women doing so many—one right after another—in ninety-plus degrees and full humidity would make up for any clumsiness. I figured that they would see us drenched in as much sincerity as sweat.

After every morning service, with a few exceptions, we would be treated to an hour or more of lecturing on some aspect of Korean Buddhism by Sunim. Haju and I would listen as best we could, stomachs growling, sitting on hard floors, covered in sweat, while the rest of the monastery—except for kitchen staff—apparently went back to bed. Sometimes even Sunim slept which was like getting a bonus because we could sneak in naps as well. Or sit in meditation for a while.

Then, breakfast. In his scholarly book titled *The Zen Monastic Experience*, Robert Buswell talks about how meals are the highlight of a monk's day: "For a monk in a large training monastery, the rigid daily schedule and disciplined training regimen do not allow much opportunity to indulge in any of the little pleasures most laypersons take for granted. There is no television to watch, no newspaper to read, no time for naps. With so few outlets for sensual indulgence (precisely the intention of the tight regime), the highlights of the day are meals, which the monks attack with great, if barely restrained, gusto." (Robert E. Buswell Jr., *The Zen Monastic Experience,* Princeton University Press, Princeton, New Jersey, 1992, p. 120)

He wasn't kidding. Meals quickly became the focal point for most of our days. Would we make it back to the monastery in time for lunch or the evening meal? I never missed a breakfast. They were the fanciest in Seoul. Rice soup, greens, peanuts for protein, tea, and kimchi. Kim-chi—spicy pickled vegetables, mostly radishes and cabbages—is Korea's national food. My experience of Koreans is that they don't just like kimchi. They love it the way Americans love pizza, the way I love Ben and Jerry's ice cream. Any flavor. "For centuries kimchi, along with rice, has made up the bulk of the Korean's diet. Rice is a staple through-out Asia, but kimchi is uniquely Korean. And kimchi is as much a part of Korean culture as is the language…" (Craig J. Brown, "Kimchi," *Morning Calm,* September, 1999, p. 38)

Kimchi is an acquired taste if you grew up on peanut butter and jelly on white bread. The first time I tried it I broke into a sweat so strong that even the backs of my knees were soaked. My nose cleared for days and I was certain I could trace all the canals from my face to my ears. After several weeks of eating it because it was the bulkiest food on some of our tables, sure enough, it became a favorite.

HOW TO MAKE KIMCHI

1. In the largest colander you have or can borrow, mix 5 to 6 cups of chopped Chinese cabbage with 6 teaspoons of sea salt. Make sure the salt is really mixed in. Forget trying to use a bowl for this. It won't work as you'll see in a minute.

2. Set the colander aside for at least 3 hours. Longer is better.

3. Rinse the cabbage thoroughly. Once you are sure it is adequately rinsed, rinse it again for good measure.

4. Drain the cabbage thoroughly.

5. Now put the cabbage in a really big bowl. Add 2 tablespoons of sugar and some crushed red chilies. With the chilies, it is a good idea to start with a couple of teaspoons, increasing the amount in small increments until you get the level of "hotness" you want. It is easy to get carried away here. Please remember that a little chili can go a long way.

6. Add $1/2$ teaspoon of chopped ginger.

7. Add 2 cloves of finely chopped garlic unless you really really love garlic. Then you can throw in an additional clove for good measure, as long as you don't mind your skin smelling like garlic for a couple of days after you eat the kimchi.

8. Add 2 finely chopped green onions.

9. Mix the whole concoction together with your hands, remembering not to rub your eyes or nose or anything else on your body for that matter. (Wash your hands thoroughly before you go to the bathroom.)

10. Let the mixture sit at room temperature for at least 2 days before serving.

11. After that, keep the kimchi in the refrigerator in tightly closed containers. It should last for as long as it takes to eat it.

Kimchi was served at every meal in the city and the mountains, as much as we could eat. Mostly it was made of Chinese cabbage but sometimes we had radishes, unidentified leaves, or cucumber (at least I think that's what it was). At one meal I was certain it was made with dandelion stems, but by then I was probably hallucinating. It was right after a dream where I had pizza and ice cream at a party, only they both tasted like kimchi. After only a few days in Seoul we smelled like kimchi; I could lick my arm and taste it.

At some of our stops we were offered special breakfasts. I tried not to think about what we were eating, trusting it to be vegetarian food. In an effort to not insult whoever had worked hard to make us the breakfast I discovered that gulping down food without breathing before or after the gulp for as long as possible made it possible to eat whatever was in front of us. But one morning I foolishly tried to figure out what foods were in a pungent bowl of soup. Having assumed I was eating vegetarian meals I was stunned to see a pileup of tiny mussel shells at the bottom of the bowl, which meant that the tiny rubber-band-like pieces floating in the broth were the mussels themselves.

What to do?

1. Eat them and try not to throw up.

2. Try to hide the rest of the soup somewhere.

3. Spill the remains on my lap—by then my pants were so filthy the rotting mussel smell wouldn't even register. I picked choice three.

Food of the Buddhas were Korean pancakes. Once or twice a plate piled high with pancakes greeted us when we all sat down. They were delicious beyond words after days without a wheat product in sight. Korean pancakes aren't sweet. Instead of fruit, slivers of vegetables are dropped into the egg, flour, and milk batter when it is ladled onto a hot frying pan. The pancakes are hot, healthy, and filling. We always ate all a cook was willing to fry.

HOW TO MAKE KOREAN PANCAKES

2 cups flour

6 eggs

**1 cup nonfat milk (actually any type of milk will probably work.
Soy milk is okay as well.)**

1 cup water

1 tablespoon safflower oil

**A couple of handfuls of raw vegetable strips: carrots, cucumbers,
whatever you feel like. Crunchy vegetables work best.**

Prepare vegetable strips by slicing the vegetables into sticks about the size
of matchsticks. Actually it is probably a good idea to cut up about twice
as many vegetables as you think you'll need because, if you are like me,
you'll end up snacking on them as you prepare the pancakes.

When you have as many vegetables as you want or have time to prepare, pour a little oil such as canola or safflower oil into a frying pan and
stir fry them for 15 to 20 seconds so they won't be too crunchy in the pancakes. Set them aside until it is time to make the pancakes.

Start out by beating everything together except the flour which should
be in a big bowl all by itself. Then make a well in the center of the flour
and add the milk, water, and oil. Beat it until it is smooth. The batter
should be pretty thin. Cover and refrigerate for at least 2 hours.

When you are ready to make the pancakes just ladle the batter onto a
hot greased frying pan the way you would with breakfast pancakes. As
soon as the batter hits the griddle gently drop a small handful of vegetable
strips on top of the batter.

Cook until the batter on the griddle gets a little bubbly and the edges
look a bit browned, then flip the pancake over. Count to about 20 and lift
up the pancake edge. If the bottom edge is golden, you are done. Eat the
first pancake just to make sure the rest will be okay for everyone else.

Makes about 36 pancakes.

Our breakfasts of rice, soup, and kimchi gave me the energy to constantly run after Sunim—to catch a bus, or a train, or through busy city streets on the way to the next mountain or monastery or errand. In fact our trip was a marathon race that began the day we dropped into Seoul and didn't stop until Haju and I got on the plane back to the United States. Our job description? Keep a beginner's mind, notice everything, and don't screw up. Scrape off ego dreck so we could experience powerful enough *samadhi* to know the pilgrimage was working its magic. (*The Shambala Dictionary of Buddhism and Zen* defines *samadhi* as "collectedness of the mind on a single object through the gradual calming of mental activity." It is a wonderful peaceful state in that the consciousness of the experiencing subject literally merges with the experienced object so there is only experience. No judgment. No opinions.) I had two extra jobs: to carry Sunim's extra money and not drop my pants' belt (attached to my pants) into the stand-up toilets. I never lost the money but gave up on trying to keep my belt clean by day three.

There were always chores related to our travelling into the mountains: tickets to get, phone calls to make, money to exchange. Then we would head back to whatever temple we were staying in, or off to the next temple, hopefully in time for lunch. Lunch at the monasteries is similar to the breakfast fare, only generally there is more of it, including more vegetable and kimchi side dishes. Each morning I found myself swearing that I would never eat rice again and every lunchtime I was grateful rice was there as the main dish. Every once in a while a special meal would come our way—instant noodles on a long bus ride or, for a party for a monk celebrating his seventieth birthday, a Western-style birthday cake.

After lunch most monks and nuns disappear to do work practice. Since we never stayed in one place long enough to be of help we only really did work practice once. A Korean student of Sunim's, facing a fall indigo harvest, needed help. We drove for hours up dirt paths into the mountains to the hut where he and his wife lived. There we spent ten hours pulling indigo leaves off their branches. By that point in the trip it was with utter relief that we sat and pulled and sat and pulled and sat and pulled instead of climbing a mountain or running after a bus or train.

On some rainy days, if it was really pouring, we found Buddhist museums or a tearoom to visit. Sunim liked checking out temple bookstores for books he couldn't get in the United States, so we got to know the insides of more than a dozen bookstores quite intimately. I was always happy to stop because it meant I could sit outside on my haunches and watch the world.

Six o'clock meant supper. Rice, kimchi, vegetables, all wolfed down in less than ten minutes. Tea. Then evening practice at 6:30. Off to the main meditation hall we would go to chant and prostrate and hope we wouldn't get yelled at by Sunim about some mistake or other. But we always were. Invariably we hadn't used our "common sense" about something—where we put our shoes, how our robes hung on our shoulders, who we bowed to and when, whether we looked at someone inappropriately—all new rules to me.

In the beginning, I just waited Sunim out. I knew he was under a lot of pressure introducing two Western women to the monks. Surprisingly, Haju's new role as dharma heir seemed to be no big deal. Most of the monks and nuns we met just bowed to her without comment. Ditto for me. For the younger monks and nuns we seemed to be a curiosity. I usually caught a couple of them staring at us at each of the temples. But there were no ceremonies, no special gifts given, no pedestals for Haju to climb.

Within days Sunim was treating both Haju and me like novice monks. In truth we were ignorant of much of the Korean protocol. Although Haju had been on a three-month pilgrimage into the mountains years ago, she had had a special guide, another woman who mentored her through the situations we now faced. This time we were without a female guide whispering advice into our ears, so we just did our best.

By 10 o'clock, it was lights out and we were all supposed to be sleeping. By this time Sunim would usually be focused on something or someone else, and, once I realized that I was NEVER going to get the rules right, this was the time I used to sneak off to sit or wash socks and underwear before they grew any more rank (a losing battle but one I was determined to fight in the name of my Irish grandmother who by now was definitely turning over in her grave at our collective filthiness).

Because it was usually too hot to sleep and we were often in teeny windowless rooms, on some nights Haju and I would get up after midnight to sit until the 3 A.M. wake up. The night-lights in the monasteries were the moon and the stars. It was fun to tiptoe around the temple complex while everyone else slept, trying to remember where the nearest bathroom was, or where I could get some water to drink.

Hunger kept me up as well. I would tiptoe out of our sleeping room and just sit outside the door looking at the sky, chewing a piece of gum in an effort to fool my stomach into a feeling of fullness so I could get some sleep. By the time the flavor of the gum was chewed out, the sounds of the young novice monks, often rising at 2:30 A.M., kept me awake thinking about everything from how crazy we all make our lives, to how fresh the mountains smelled, to trying to remember what day it was and which temple we were in.

I loved the nights. The quiet. The sounds of insects serenading each other. Usually the sound and smell of rushing water nearby. I loved how the novice monks always knew I was sitting outside of my room even though it was dark and always looked up, smiled, and made little waves as they tiptoed by. I even enjoyed listening to Haju and Kaeo taking turns snoring, grateful that for once it wasn't me.

Every once in a while, wrapped in the quiet, it felt like the moon—so close—was sneaking up on me because it wanted to sit too. It was good company. Sometimes I would promise myself to just sit outside for a couple of minutes only to wake up to the sound of the *moktak*. Sometimes the moon and I would just sit together until it was time to formally prepare for the day.

Daily life in the monasteries, surrounded by unknown rules and a completely foreign culture, forced a massive shift in focus. Lost was any ability to be the best. Gone was any trace of attractiveness. Nothing remained of pride in knowing how things are done. In their place, humility, and a growing determination to keep my initial resolve to simply be with all our experiences, whatever form they took. By the time we reached the mountains it was clear that Haju and I were going to be so clumsy compared to Sunim and Kaeo, that to practice "just this" would be a major accomplishment.

Sometimes, just when I would finally feel angry after one of Sunim's shouting binges or too tired to climb one more mountain when the last one was supposed to be the end of the day, and I would ask myself again, "Why am I here?" there would be a magic moment.

Here's one of them. At the end of an afternoon filled with errands in Seoul, Sunim suddenly started staring into the tiny alleyways that branched off of the main road where we were walking. Without warning he turned into one, the three of us following like puppies. Just when it looked like we were about to reach a dead end, there was an exit—a smaller alley too small for cars. We followed that to a third one, which led us to a different main street. Glancing up and down the street, Sunim looked up at the high-rise on the corner to our left and immediately started walking down some stairs into its basement. At the bottom there were more alleys that became corridors. First we went left. Then right. Then left again. I wished I had bread crumbs to make sure we would find our way back to our starting point. Suddenly Sunim stopped. We were facing a tiny shop window with its blinds drawn. There was a small sign on the door.

Sunim opened the door.

We were looking into a Korean version of a 1950s diner. Two old men were chatting away in one of the dozen or so booths that filled the room.

In another booth an older man and woman faced each other over a foot-high pile of chestnuts. They were peeling them, throwing the shells into a huge bucket and the peeled chestnuts into a quart bowl on the table. At the front of the room a counter was crammed full of jars of what looked like tea, and a handful of industrial-size blenders. The walls were laced with pictures of mountain scenes, local art work, and health posters.

Sunim nodded at the couple. The woman motioned us into a booth, got up, walked behind the counter, and five minutes later appeared with four huge cups of steaming…oil? She set one in front of each of us. She left and then came back with four small plates. Each one held two peeled chestnuts and a couple of gingko berries.

I stared at my cup. The liquid was thick, almost purple black, and syrupy. It looked like the oil I got out of my old Volvo the first and last time I ever tried doing my own oil change. It even smelled like the oil. I knew we were expected to drink every drop of whatever it was.

The old men had stopped their conversation to watch us. As I leaned over to pick up the cup I noticed pale whitish lumps floating around just under the surface. They looked like bones. Taking time to remind myself that Sunim would definitely not order us bone tea, I took a huge gulp.

Imagine cough syrup heated to scalding, with a touch of molasses and maybe whiskey thrown in for good measure—and a handful of dried apple pieces. That's what we were drinking. Sunim said it would keep us healthy on the pilgrimage. Looking back, I think he meant that it would coat our intestines so thickly that germs would be helpless against it. Like tequila, by the third gulp the tea tasted just fine. By the end of the cup I was convinced it had magic powers. My body felt light and my worries were gone. When we finished the proprietress gave each of us a frothy cup of rice and tomato juice to drink down like a shot of whiskey. It would protect us from being lonely and depressed while travelling, Sunim said.

Another magic moment occurred when we turned a corner of a mountain crest to see the most beautiful vista I have ever seen or could ever have imagined. Row upon row of soft blue and purple mountaintops spread out as far as we could see. It was like the top of a bumpy quilt that stretched all the way to the heavens. On the same mountains we stopped for some green tea in a tiny hermitage that was literally carved into the side of a cliff. It just happened to be a hermitage where my favorite wildly eccentric monk, Wonhyo, had spent a lot of his time centuries ago. I got to sit where he had sat and drink tea that was probably pretty close to the tea he drank. It was the ultimate groupie experience.

Sometimes the magic moments surfaced in the form of stories. At a Seoul temple we were told the story of a laywoman, a business owner who, when she died, donated her house as a temple, "For the benefit of all beings." Her will instructed that her head be shaved and her body dressed in robes so she would be reborn as a monk. The monks at her temple tease each other over which one is her, reborn. A picture of a monk on the wall of Sunim's bedroom in Seoul provoked another story. Hyobong Sunim was a brilliant university student in the 1920s before he became a judge in the Japanese penal system that ruled Korea. "Serving Japanese imperialism" was very difficult for him. The breaking point came when he gave someone a death sentence on evidence that was so slim that he became haunted by his own decision. So he resigned. He walked out. Nobody could believe he had the guts and everyone expected that he would be hunted down and executed. But somehow he never was. Instead he became a travelling candy man selling taffies to children, eventually ending up at the Seoul temple as a monk. By this time he was in his late forties. In Korea, people who enter the monasteries at an older age are often put down as having been tainted by worldly experience. Not this guy. When he sat, he would meditate for hours, sit until he got blisters on his rear end—earning the name of "stone mortar" and gaining the respect of all of the temple's monks then and now.

But the magic moments were rare. Mostly we faced a tough sweat-covered reality, day and night. It dripped into our eyes and off the tip of our noses. In intense heat and humidity we were travelling by foot wearing tee shirts, socks, and heavy cotton robes—carrying 20 to 30 pounds worth of the books that kept finding Sunim. Windowless sleeping rooms became saunas. The mats we slept on were soaked by sweat by morning. It was hard at times not to be just plain pissed off from the constant, intense discomfort.

With each passing day the rules came at us fast and furious. We were eating food so spicy it made our noses drip like faucets, but we were told not to blow our noses. Don't point at anyone. Don't laugh or show emotion. Always bow back whenever someone bows in your direction.

I vaguely remember telling myself in the first week that the pilgrimage would probably be tough but that we would all do fine. Not a single heart palpitation marred the landscape. I had lived with rules before and heat was just heat. Besides we were only going for a month. How hard could it get?

The rest of the pilgrimage taught me the futility of making predictions when travelling with Zen masters.

Chapter Five

Into the Mountains

Journal entry: August 26, 1999, Seoul

"If I don't write in this—almost by the hour—I'll never remember each day. They are so packed full of small and large moments. Today's start: 4 A.M. after a restless night of sweating and kamikaze mosquito attacks. I'm amazed at how fast I've learned to live on so little sleep. After 108 prostrations in a beautiful Buddha hall we did *Yebul* and sat while the monks gonged and drummed the world awake. Between waking and breakfast, about three hours, we visited a temple down the street... It's clear we'll be doing a lot of "waiting here, waiting there" practice on this trip. Okay. Wish there wasn't a rule that we can only wash every ten days. It's bad enough to travel without deodorant. Same clothes, same smell, day and night. Only more rank with each passing day. In this heat and humidity we're almost moldy by day three. Definitely by day four. Outward Bound is for wimps compared to this."

On August 29 we left for the Chiri Mountains, first to Taegu by bus for four hours. Then a local bus took us on an hour and a half climb up to Heinsa. The ride offered an opportunity to consider the dynamics of the four of us travelling together. Remembering Sunim once telling us at a retreat to "just do the obvious in any difficult situation," I suddenly thought of a hilarious story someone once told me about being observant. It was about Sir William Osler, a professor of medicine at Oxford

University. He was giving a lecture on the importance of paying attention. To emphasize his point he suddenly picked up a bottle, telling the
students that the bottle contained a urine sample. Opening it, he stated
that it is often possible to determine the disease someone has by tasting
the contents. He dipped his finger into the fluid, put it into his mouth,
and passed the bottle to the first student. "Each of you please do exactly
as I did. Perhaps we can learn the importance of this technique and
diagnose the case."

Row by row, student after student poked a finger into the bottle and
bravely sampled the contents. When the bottle made it back to Dr. Osler
he just looked at the students. If they had really paid attention the way he
instructed them to they would have noticed that he put his index finger
in the bottle and his middle finger in his mouth.

Determined not to spend the rest of the pilgrimage with the wrong
finger in my mouth, I vowed to pay better attention. I would do just what
Sunim did, following his footsteps as closely as possible. When he bowed
I would bow, when he picked up a teacup, I would pick up a teacup.
When he moved, I would move. Haju must have been thinking similar
thoughts because she suggested that she and I stop talking to each other
in an effort to pay better attention and make the most of the trip. Instant
agreement on my part.

* * *

When it became obvious to Koreans that marauders were going to be
a permanent fixture on their historical landscape, they decided they
needed to provide special attention to the scriptures they were housing.
Heinsa was the temple that took on that responsibility since it was
Korea's "protected" temple. In fact, the reason it had been built in the first
place was because two monks had saved the queen's life (the wife of King
Aejang, ruler from 800-809 A.D.) by tying one end of a piece of string to
a tumor she had, tying the other to a tree, and chanting until her tumor

disappeared. I swear I am not making this up. In gratitude the king built the two monks a temple. They named it Heinsa, which means "reflection on the smooth sea."

Heinsa is a half-hour walk up a lovely tree-shaded mountain road from the bus stop. Walking into the compound is like walking into a thousand-year-old storybook. The steps are huge stones, the halls are massive handcrafted buildings, so colorful, with painted patterns so intricate, they must have taken a millennium to paint. Enormous gold statues fill the main hall, surrounded by flowers, fruit, and detailed paintings from Buddha's life. Behind the main hall, up a flight of stairs so steep you have to climb them like you'd climb a mountain, are two long buildings that have the most pungent wood smell your nose will experience in this lifetime. That's because they are filled with more than 83,400 wooden blocks, each the size of a high school chemistry textbook, that are inscribed with the entire Buddhist scripture (Tripitaka) in Korean.

It took two tries to get all of the scriptures written and stored in one place. On the first try, the monks spent seventy-seven years carving the white birch. But the Mongols burned the blocks in 1232. The second time it only took sixteen years to inscribe all the blocks since the monks had the carving technique down. Each block was soaked in sea water for three years to preserve the wood before it was carved. Then the blocks were boiled in salted water and dried in the shade so they would last for years and years, or until the next invasion anyway. When you look at them lined up on the shelves five layers in each row, they look like a sea of wooden rulers marching off to war.

* * *

Heinsa was so unexpectedly beautiful that I couldn't imagine how other temples could be any prettier. It was as though a stone fairyland had grown right out of the mountain. Everything was spotlessly clean, from the dirt courtyards we wandered in to the water cisterns we drank from.

Color was everywhere, from tiny flowers popping up in rock crevices to the splashes of color filling the different meditation halls.

The temple buildings in the compound had wall-to-wall primary colored doors covered with intricate patterns of flowers, circles, and clouds. Even the eaves under the roofs were painted in a rainbow of colors. Tiled rooftops looked like bird wings about to unfold. Inside the halls huge golden Buddhas held court, backed by floor-to-ceiling paintings of Bodhisattvas. Because of all the wooden scriptures an earthy, musty smell follows you everywhere, one like your grandparents' old house on the farm you used to visit when you were a kid.

From Heinsa we rushed to Pulguksa, with some high mountain climbing in between. Having favorites is a dangerous thing in a spiritual tradition where strong opinions are the mark of a hopelessly unenlightened mind. Oh well. Of all the temples we visited I liked Pulguksa best. The temple has the most exquisite stone stairways standing on the earth today. They are actually called bridges because it is believed that they lead visitors away from the mundane world into the gates of paradise, or at least an enlightened life. Even the number of steps on each bridge is meaningful. For example on the Lotus Flower Bridge there are ten steps symbolizing the human longings we need to let go of if we are to enter paradise. The opening under the staircase, shaped like a rainbow, represents our wish to reach the peace of understanding life, death, and everything in between. Each stone bridge is so beautiful you want to get married, even if you are waist deep in the land of monks, just so you can walk down them in a long flowing pearl-colored silk gown with a ten-foot train and lots of lace. And the stone walls! Huge boulders form bases topped with amazingly intricate patterns of stone crosses and smaller rocks. One of Pulguksa's walls has actually been named the most beautiful stone wall in the world. Rounded tile roofs seem to grow right out of the walls. Even their overhangs are painted with detailed rainbow-colored designs and that doesn't begin to describe the shrines inside the temple's gates.

Your eyes get so tired of gaping at all the beauty that, after a while, you yearn for a pile of trash to stare at. Really. Anything to stop the constant exclamations of awe coming out of your mouth.

* * *

Pulguksa was built in 528 A.D., the year after Buddhism was officially accepted by the Silla dynasty during the reign of King Beophung. Many of Korea's most famous monks have spent time there, both before and after the temple was destroyed by the Japanese in 1592 and later rebuilt. One of the pagodas in its central square looks like a huge square five-layer wedding cake topped by a shish kebob, and holds the ashes of eight Buddhist saints in it. At least that's what the Koreans believed until the pagoda was taken apart to be repaired in 1966. Inside the workmen found a huge sutra, the Great Mantra Sutra, as well as seventy other important relics.

All of the temples have stories. Wonderful ones. The kind of stories best heard by a campfire when it's cold enough to make you lean into its warmth and late enough to stop your rational mind from wondering whether the story could possibly be true. Pulguksa has one of the most romantic ones. Historically when young Korean men were asked to help build a temple, part of the deal was that they had to completely give up their worldly life while the temple was under construction. In other words no women, no alcohol, no smoking, no TV, no Matchmaker.com. The workers who suffered the most were the ones who had the misfortune of falling in love right before they entered the temple grounds to begin the project. Since no one ever knew how long a project would take—sometimes several years—leaving a lover behind could be excruciatingly painful. And since the men, at least in the olden days, also had to promise that they wouldn't communicate with anyone outside of the temple while they were working, the family and friends left behind learned to watch for clues that would tell them how a project was going. One of those clues was shadows. The size of the shadow a building cast showed how much work was left to do.

Well, there was a young mason named Asadal who came from the southwestern part of the peninsula up to the mountains to help build the pagodas on Pulguksa's grounds. Unfortunately he had to leave his young wife, Asanyo, alone, promising her that he would return to her the minute the pagodas were completed. After years of waiting for her beloved, Asanyo made her own journey to Pulguksa to find out if her husband was still alive. Since no outsiders were allowed inside the temple grounds she was stopped at the first gate. A kindly old monk, seeing her distress, told her to wait beside a nearby pond and to watch the pond. When the pagodas were completed she would see them reflected in the water.

Asanyo waited and waited until one day, completely heartbroken because she still saw no reflection in the pond, she threw herself into the water and drowned herself. That was where her husband found her the very next day. His craftsmanship had been so exquisite that the pagoda had never cast a shadow—even when it was finished. To this day it is still called "The Pagoda Without Reflection." Asadal was so heartbroken by the death of his wife he was never seen again, but I swear I could feel Asadal walking through the grounds.

* * *

By the time we reached Pulguksa I had perfected the technique of taking a twenty-second ice-cold shower while jumping up and down on my dirty clothes that were piled into a huge plastic bowl filled with ordinary soap and water. The effort got the worst of the grime out. Drying clothes on my body kept me cool. I told myself that lugging around books for Sunim was simply the much needed upper-body strength training I had been wanting to do.

Things were also getting a bit surreal by this time. One day while we were visiting a young artist monk, Sunim suddenly told us to perform for him. Haju spontaneously made up a poem while I pretended to be a dying swan. We finished up our improv act splayed on the floor, laughing ourselves silly. Later, during a very long bus trip, we stopped for a ten-minute "noodle break" where I stood in a line behind a teenage boy wearing a sweatshirt announcing that "Jesus died for your shins." Thank goodness! Upon our arrival in another city, Sunim instructed me to do summersaults on a ceremonial mound to honor the ancient monks and nuns. Later, we even tried hitchhiking our way out of one of the shrines we visited. We were living the pilgrimage moment-to-moment, sometimes completely clueless about where our next night would be spent or how we would get from one temple to another.

* * *

There's a Zen saying, "You can piece together three pounds of fleas but you can't piece together three monks." Climbing the mountains, rushing from temple to temple, our differences surfaced and then hardened. Kaeo shifted into a formal samurai monk mode. Haju somehow drifted off into her own world, always trying to please Sunim, sometimes crying when we were scolded. I got angry as Sunim's moods started to darken with every passing monastery.

In the mountains Sunim's behavior changed from a mostly compassionate, sometimes irritable older brother to a ferocious tiger. He rushed in front of us up the paths until we could no longer see him, leaving us unsure which forks to take. Sometimes he would send Kaeo—who kept up with him despite the sixty pounds of books, video equipment, and robes he was carrying—back to yell at us to hurry up. And Kaeo yelled, but always with a grin on his face unless he was tired. At one point on the way up to Pulguksa he grabbed my backpack and pulled half of Haju's stuff out of hers. We were both carrying two backpacks stuffed with Sunim's books. He loaded the extra things into mine. Carrying the extra weight I fell farther and farther behind the group. Kaeo kept yelling at me to catch up, to do better. He insisted that my pack wasn't heavy, which was probably true if you are a six-foot, physically fit martial arts black belt army monk. He even said that my backpack was lighter than Haju's who had said, "What's in this? Rocks?" as she helped me hoist it onto my shoulders because I wasn't strong enough to lift it by myself. My job was to take care of Haju, no matter what, Kaeo said. I yelled back at him that I was doing the best I could and why did we need to rush? But there was no answer. Just heavy rain and more uphill climbs.

The lectures from Sunim multiplied. And so did the orders. "Go faster!" "Look down!" "Why are you so messy?!" "Pay attention!" When we sat on a wooden porch floor to rest, he roared, "What are you doing keeping your shoes on there?!" (Not another shoe in sight for visual clues.) "Just wait!" "Just sit there!" Evidently we were the clumsiest people he had ever brought to Korea! How could we be so clumsy? How could Haju's backpack always be so crooked?! Why couldn't I ever keep my *kasa* straight? (*Kasas* are dark brown bibs sewn from twenty-five pieces of cloth to look like tilled fields. Typically they are worn by novice monks. I figured making us wear them was Sunim's way of forewarning the monastics that we weren't up on all the protocol. But they ended up being one more reason for him to yell at us.)

If I refilled a glass of water during lunch, he would yell, "Why did you do that? Don't refill your own glass!" He kept up an ongoing diatribe about how Haju had screwed up on robe measurements for friends back home. Whenever we sat down on benches (thrilled to be on furniture, rather than the hard ground) he complained that we "spread things around too much."

We heard a constant stream of corrections whether we were climbing up mountains in the heat and pouring rain or riding the countless buses. Even while we were enveloped in a scene of breathtaking beauty, Sunim complained and scolded. Only very occasionally did it stop. At Heinsa, looking straight up the mountain that seemed at first to be sheer rock and pines, tiny beautiful monasteries popped out of the landscape as our focus sharpened. The sounds of monks chanting bounced from mountaintop to mountaintop. Finally he was quiet. No yelling.

I was so caught up in trying to do the correct thing that I was barely aware of the climb to the little hermitage called "Learning to Be Content" at the top of the mountain. All I know is that by the time we got there it felt as though we had climbed to the top of the world. The rocks surrounding us went straight up like gothic cathedral walls. Beyond the trees were a series of mountains marching off into the distance that looked like small caps of pale gray whipped cream.

The temple itself was literally built into a small cliff on the top of a peak, with stone paths leading everywhere and not an inch of space wasted. One giant step out of the "bathroom" put you face to face with a rust colored granite slab about twelve feet wide and eight feet tall. Birds were everywhere, welcoming us. We had entered a heaven realm. The rooms we slept in were tiny—if you spread three sleeping bags out in a row they took up all the space. There wasn't any furniture, only a ceiling light and some hooks on the walls for robes. A system for heating the varnished yellow paper *ondol* floors from underneath guaranteed the rooms never got cold, even when the temperatures dropped below freezing.

When we woke up the next morning it was pitch black. The only way to find the meditation hall was to follow the sound of the *moktak*, taking care to stay on the narrow wooden walkways built into the sides of the buildings. Following a morning service that echoed off the stone mountaintops, I wondered what might possibly be available for breakfast. We were so high up and we hadn't passed a single garden on our climb. I hadn't seen any roads for cars. I figured there would be rice. There was. When we entered the kitchen, ducking to get through the doorway, huge bowls of it were waiting for us. Beside them was a smorgasbord of what looked like tree leaves, twigs, and weeds. The tree leaves (a mountain version of pita bread) were used for wrapping small balls of rice and red paste. We were told that the weeds were herbs to build our immune systems. All of the greens had been gathered from the side of the mountain. Combined with some spices it was a delicious and surprisingly filling meal.

On our way back to our rooms I stumbled into a quiet moment and a chair. It was a perfect moment for haiku:

The rocks leap at us.
Birds sing good morning at dawn.
I miss M & Ms.

The mountain hermitage offered our first formal meeting with a Zen master. Iltal Sunim flat out looked like Yoda, wearing a pair of oversized glasses like the ones you buy at state fairs. He only sees people he wants to see, so it was a good thing we could offer him information about Western culture. He had spent most of his life at Heinsa and now he was interested in being reborn in the West.

Iltal was my first experience of enlightened Zen. He was completely alert. His eyes missed nothing as they swept over us. Clear. Every sentence that came out of his mouth (at least the ones that were translated for us... Oh why didn't I learn Korean?) was like a line out of a sutra. Here's a taste: "Everything is impermanent. Just live like the wind so you don't get caught in a net." Iltal told us to stay in the moment, to pay attention to what matters and to ignore everything else. Everything. That was the key to a fruitful pilgrimage. If we ignored everything but our own practice it wouldn't matter if people prostrated to us or walked away from us. It wouldn't matter if we had four hours of sleep or eight hours. Our moods wouldn't matter. I vowed to do everything I knew how to do to stay true to his advice.

Chapter Six

Tongdosa and Beyond

Journal entry: September 5, 1999, Pomosa

"Sooner or later you just cry. It's a combination of sheer exhaustion, withdrawal from all the foods you know, fatigue from squatting over holes in the ground to pee, and the discomfort—if you are a total control freak like me—of having someone else totally driving your days, minute by minute. Tongdosa was so hard for us. Sunim was tense because every mistake we made reflected back on him. Since I only know a little about Korean temple protocol it felt like every time I turned around Sunim or Kaeo was correcting me. 'Put your kasa in your room!' 'Don't put the (ant-infested) fruit plate outside your door. Keep it inside.' (They were biting ants. I was covered with welts for a week.) 'Don't talk to the monks!' One young monk, 'monk asshole' (oh dear, this trip *is* wearing), hunted us down to scold us. Then we had to do prostrations to him and he came after us even more. He said our posture sucked. We should be sitting in half lotus or full lotus. And then there's having to kneel on a hard floor for anywhere from a half hour to two hours while Sunim chats away with one of the senior monks, with no interpretation offered... I can do about thirty minutes... We're getting up at 3 A.M. and on top of that waking ourselves up at 1 A.M. or 2 A.M. to do extra practice... I can't believe I'm not hallucinating. Or maybe I am. Maybe I just have to rub my eyes and I'll be home watching *Ally McBeal* being her adorable neurotic self."

The farther we went into the mountains the more difficult the pilgrimage became. Sunim's anger was constant, whether at a distance or right up in our faces. I wanted to protect Haju but I couldn't. I wanted to protect myself but I couldn't. I wanted to pretend that we weren't getting yelled at by this furious monk. But I couldn't.

Journal entry: September 8, 1999, Yongwonsa

"Sunim keeps going after Haju for mistakes she makes—it's pretty constant. I make lots as well but he doesn't come after me as hard. She just takes it. This morning though—whew! She missed a special birthday *Yebul* (chant) at 11 A.M. where we all did prostrations for the head monk's seventieth birthday. Haju was nowhere to be found. Kaeo and I both went looking for her. Sunim was fit to be tied. When she did show up we were heading for lunch. As soon as we had finished eating our rice and vegetables Sunim made me and Haju get up from the lunch table without eating the special birthday cake that had been sent up the mountain on their pulley system. I think the *posalnims* (the handful of women living in the temple who were responsible for cooking and cleaning) felt sorry for us because they brought us fruit.

Sunim is being a real grinch. I wonder what it is. Lack of sleep? Our clumsiness? All day today correcting, correcting—most of the trip actually, with moments of respite when he teaches us about some aspect of Korean Buddhism or buys us a treat of orange juice or ice cream. I've only seen him openly grin one time—at the beginning of the trip. I hope he's okay. Anyway, it's quite an experience travelling with him."

It was heartbreaking actually. Knowing that the pilgrimage would be physically grueling, I expected Sunim to be our constant shepherd because he knew the rules, the protocol, the landscape. He was supposed to guide us through the tough parts. Maybe there would be some yelling but it would be the exception not the rule. Instead we faced daily anger, and a dispassionate meanness that shocked me to my bones.

I kept looking for clues as to how to deal with him. Surely the answer wasn't to reflect his fury. It was impossible to ignore Sunim's anger. What to do?

Teachings popped up everywhere to help. At a bus stop one day I opened an English language tourist guide to Korean temples. Right smack in the middle was a piece of paper with a teaching called the "Ten Guides along the Path" on it. It is a perfect and vivid example of crazy wisdom, making the case for conflict, ill health, and miserable moments as powerful doors to enlightenment. Very helpful if you are trying to visit more than two dozen temples in wilting heat and humidity and your sneakers are disintegrating by the minute. It goes something like this:

1. Why hope for perfect health? Perfect health leads only to greater greed. Treat illness as medicine, not disease.

2. Why long for a life free from hardship? Such a life leads only to haughtiness and self-pampering. Make worries and hardships a way of life.

3. Why hope for a lack of impediments in your study? Release is hiding right behind obstructions.

4. Why hope for a lack of temptations in your training? A lack of temptations will only soften your resolve. Treat temptations as friends who are helping you along the way.

5. Why hope for easy success? Easy accomplishment leads only to increased rashness. Accomplish through difficulties.

6. Why hope to get your way with friends? Having friends give in to your wishes only leads to arrogance. Make long-term friends through compromise in your relationships.

7. Why expect people to follow your wishes or commands? This, too, leads to arrogance. Consider those who differ with you to be your character builders.

8. Why expect rewards for your kindnesses? This leads only to a scheming mind.

9. Why expect more of your life than you deserve? Exaggerated profit seeking leads only to foolishness. Become rich at heart with small amounts.

10. Why complain about vexations? This leads only to resentment and poison in the heart. Consider vexations as the first door on the path.

(*Korean Buddhism*, published by the Korean Buddhist Chogye Order, Seoul Korea, 1996, p. 115)

If you spend any time in Tongdosa, which was our next stop, it is helpful to keep these guides in mind. Rules there are strict, discipline is pervasive, and foreigners are barely tolerated. It's hard, at first, to see the sheer beauty of the place. Happily though, once any "vexations" are embraced, Tongdosa dances the dance of the ancients. The complex is calm, almost eerie, and has a tangible cloud of holiness. Even the name adds to the aura of the temple. Translated into English it is "Pass into Enlightenment," which I found encouraging at a moment when I most needed it.

* * *

As one of the three jewel temples of Korea, Tongdosa represents the presence of the Buddha to wayfarers. As the story goes, Tongdosa was built in 646 A.D. during the reign of one of the only truly supportive Korean monarchs, Queen Sondok. She was partially motivated by her relationship to the monk who built the temple, Master Cha-jang. I think he was her cousin. Anyway, Cha-jang went to China to study under Buddhist masters there, bringing actual relics back with him. On his return to Korea he demonstrated such a skill at administration that the king asked him to join the court. Several times. After a series of refusals the king commanded Cha-jang to join his administration, telling him he would be killed if he refused again. Cha-jang's response? He refused anyway. You have to admire the man's courage.

Dumbfounded, the king asked him why, since dying by order of the king was about as awful a situation as anyone might face. Cha-jang's reply? "I would rather be keeping the laws of the Buddha for one day than live for one hundred years breaking them." Struck by the monk's reply the king backed off and supported Cha-jang's work at the temple from then on.

It's hard to tell exactly what Tongdosa looked like in its earliest years since, like Heinsa, it was destroyed by the Japanese in 1592. Now, however, it is the largest temple compound in the country, consisting of thirty-five of your typically breathtakingly beautiful buildings. They, in turn, are surrounded by smaller "spin off" hermitages tucked in the nooks and crannies of the valleys behind the temple.

What makes Tongdosa memorable, in addition to its discipline and red biting ants, is that it is the one temple we visited that doesn't have a Buddha statue in its main hall. Compared with the Buddha-filled halls in the other temples, this took some getting used to. Your eyes want to see a Buddha, and if you just happen to be travelling on little sleep you'll probably hallucinate one in an effort to avoid having to use any extra energy trying to figure out what the heck is missing.

Instead of statues, Tongdosa has an open courtyard about the size of a baseball diamond behind the main hall. It is surrounded by waist-high stone fences. Sitting in the middle of the courtyard is a stupa where some of Buddha's relics are believed to be enshrined. Even when the temple grounds are filled with visitors there is a hush surrounding the courtyard. You can just feel the thousands and thousands of monks and nuns who have circled the stupa for centuries, chanting for peace and wisdom.

* * *

We arrived at Tongdosa at the end of a long, tough day. The first monk we met was not going to let us stay. Sunim insisted that we had traveled far and deserved rooms. We went to sleep early. In the morning the sheer glow of the meditation hall reignited a determination to simply live inside my practice. Sunim could be as grouchy as he pleased, and so could the rest of the monks if they felt so inclined. I would just stay immersed in equanimity—even if it killed me.

And it just might, I realized. I felt schizophrenic. There we were, deep in the land of the patriarchs: one minute, I was sighing with happiness from the beauty and the sheer wonder of being in the temple. The next minute I was scratching bite welts until they bled. The next I was looking down at my feet while Sunim found something else we had done wrong.

Later, at home, reading an essay by Robert Thurman, who has perhaps the deepest understanding of Buddhism East meets Buddhism West, I thought about how I had done the unthinkable. I had put all my marbles in the wrong basket. Instead of taking refuge in Buddha, dharma, and sangha, and me, I had handed everything over to Sunim:

"There was the idea that authority figures—particularly Asian—could provide magic roads to enlightenment by dependency and devotion to them. This led to a tremendous amount of abuse, a lot of dependency, a lot of people burning out, a lot of people spending years meditating the wrong way. The caution there was the underestimation of the power of the authoritarian personality structure in the Judeo-Christian Western mind, whether people think they're secularists or not, and the tendency to focus that authoritarian dependency on a particular group." (*New Age Journal*, November/December, 1999, p. 139)

But Thurman was later. In Korea I was in the belly of the beast on unknown mountains with unfathomable rules, face to face with a dragon. In other words, I was screwed.

Fortunately, help keeping my vow showed up in some wildly creative forms. In an old, old book in one of the monk's rooms I literally stumbled into the "Ten Diseases of Meditation Practice," which provided a clear explanation for my own inability to take refuge in dharma when things got tough. Here are the diseases:

1. Entertaining thoughts of "is" or "is not." (There I was categorizing everyone and everything. She is holy. He is not. He is a good monk. He is not a good monk.)

2. Thinking Zhaozhou said "no" because in reality there is just nothing. (A reference to a famous Zen koan about whether a dog has Buddha nature. Does one?)

3. Resorting to principles or theories. (I most definitely had theories and principles on the brain, all going at full throttle.)

4. Trying to resolve the *hwadu* (koan) as an object of intellectual inquiry. (Cringe. Intellectual inquiry is my life. And then some.)

5. When the master raises his eyebrows or blinks his eyes taking such things as indicators regarding the meaning of dharma. (There I was, watching Sunim's every move. We were both goners.)

6. Regarding the skillful use of words as a means to express the truth.

7. Regarding a state of vacuity and ease for realization of the truth. (I would have gladly entertained a state of vacuity and ease given the chance. It beat survival mode.)

8. Taking the place where you become aware of sense objects to be the mind. (A blunt reminder that I was putting my energy into the wrong stuff.

9. Relying upon words quoted from the teachings. (I already knew that didn't work, having tried. Maybe someday knowledge will be the same as wisdom. Sigh.)

10. Remaining in a deluded state waiting for enlightenment to happen. (Ditto on this one. Having waited more than forty years, it was clear that being an active player in the whole mess was the only way out of my misery.)

Light bulb after light bulb went off. I was reacting to all the wrong things, to things that ultimately didn't matter because they were just distractions. In the end there was no difference between Sunim's anger and a master's eyebrows twitching. (Come to think of it, his eyebrows did twitch!) I was trying desperately to resort to principles and theories, to my own definition of what a good Zen master should be. I was still trying to rely on the teachings, trying to lose myself in them when I could so the trip wouldn't be so painful. I was wallowing in how mistreated we were, especially Haju, listing all the failings of Sunim—pages of them on a good day—missing the whole point. That was what I yearned for: a clear, grounded, heartfilled awareness was behind all of it. It was behind the words, the reactions, the judgment. Once again I vowed to just do practice, to just be practice. Forget the rules whispered into my ear by Kaeo who was trying to keep me out of trouble. Haju would be okay without my unskilled efforts to be a buffer. She's been with Sunim for a quarter of a century; she knows what he's like.

Legends of heroic efforts helped me as well. How dare I be miserable in the face of the kind of effort put in by so many of the monks and nuns who made pilgrimages in these mountains over the centuries before us? Their stories offered some sort of phantom dharma gasoline that I pumped into my system, giving me patience, a wider perspective, and faith.

Pusol was one of those monks. Born in 647, Pusol apparently showed signs of spiritual yearnings at an early age. Like Shakyamuni Buddha, as a child Pusol would often sit for hours staring at the sky or tucked into mountain bushes quietly waiting out the day. By the age of five he entered Pulguksa as a young monk, and began his formal study of Buddhist scriptures at age seven. By the time he was a teen, Pusol was ready to explore the larger world, having decided that monastery life was too constricting. With two best friends, Yongjo and Yonghi, he made a pilgrimage to the Crown-of-Heaven mountain. There the three proceeded to build a hut to live in. They stayed three years, subsisting on pine pollen and water. From there they moved to the Chiri Mountains, where we were travelling. For ten years the three lived in complete silence. One day they each composed a poem to express the joy of their lives. Yongjo went first:

The quiet place we occupied
Was but a hut in a tree lined mountain pass.

Oneness cultivated through meditation
The Ultimate Way attained, rejoicing followed.

Who will recognize the unearthed jade?
The bird who picked a flower sings merrily by itself.

Desolate and deserted, no affairs to attend to;
The single taste of dharma penetrates my whole being.

Yonghi went next:

On the meditation hut of old pine trees, the moon shines
As clouds disperse on the peaks of joy.

How often have I sharpened my wisdom sword?
More than twice the origin of mind revealed itself.

Though spring is yet early and desolate,
Mountain buds twitter from early morning.

All partake in the joy of the Unborn.
No need to break through the gate of the Patriarchs.

Finally, Pusol:

Practicing dharma that transcended both stillness and emptiness
We lived together in a hut where clouds and cranes became our
friends.

Having realized the non-dual is no other
than absolute liberation,
Whom shall I ask about (immeasurable and infinite)?

Leisurely I look at the lovely flowers blossoming in the garden,
Unmindfully I listen to the birds singing by the window.

Enter the state of a Tathagata directly,
Why trouble yourself piling up practice?

(Poems taken from "Buddhist Tales From the Land of Morning Calm: Layman Pusol" by Samu Sunim, in *Spring Wind Buddhist Cultural Forum*, Volume 4, #3, Fall, 1984, pp. 22-26)

Poems completed, the three climbed down the mountain and decided to travel north. During a rainstorm they took refuge at the home of Mr. and Mrs. No Resentment. (Great name. If I ever get another dog I think I'll name her No Resentment.) The No Resentments had a daughter named Wonderful Flower. (Good name for a white cat.) She was eighteen years old, beautiful, and mute—the daughter, not the cat. When she heard Pusol speak about the dharma she began to sob. When Wonderful Flower finally stopped crying she spoke for the first time in her life. Her words? "I must marry Pusol! We must become husband and wife! I will serve him forever in this life and beyond."

Talk about a shock! Totally embarrassed, her parents dragged Wonderful Flower out of the room, admonishing her for uttering such nonsense. Unmoved, the young woman declared that she would kill herself if Pusol didn't marry her.

The three monks decided to leave. Seeing this, Wonderful Flower threw herself on the ground in front of Pusol, clinging to his leg. Her parents, frantic, begged Pusol to save their daughter.

"Pusol, who remained unmoved up to this point, now realized that if he left he would be hurting not one person but three, for Mr. and Mrs. No Resentment would not live long if anything disastrous happened to their daughter. He thought about his cultivation of the way. All along his spiritual practice had been to free himself from all attachments in order to reveal the original mind. Now suddenly he was faced with creating a bond that would chain him to the world." (*Spring Wind,* p. 27)

So he stayed. (His friends thought he was nuts.)

Pusol and Wonderful Flower married. Pusol took care of Mr. and Mrs. No Resentment as though they were his own parents. Although gardening and farming were new to him he worked hard, continuing his habit of getting up at 3 A.M. each day. Instead of a Buddha statue he found two stones—one almost five times bigger than the other—and, laying one on top of the other, used them as a stone Buddha.

Every morning Pusol would offer a bowl of water to the stone Buddha and then sit in meditation until daybreak. But one morning, when his wife reached over to hug him in her sleep and he wasn't there, all hell broke loose. Opening her eyes she saw him doing prostrations in the dark. She was furious! Screaming at Pusol that it was time to stop pretending he was a monk, she picked up the stone Buddha and heaved it outside.

Pusol's reaction? He decided that Wonderful Flower was a Buddha. He would just do prostrations and meditate before her. Easy. So he began slipping out of bed at night to do prostrations to his wife. Then he would sit. Until one morning when Wonderful Flower opened her eyes to see her husband sitting in meditation right in front of her. She could have touched his nose with her tongue. This time, instead of fury, Wonderful Flower felt fear. Convinced that Pusol had gone completely insane she started crying. When Pusol tried to comfort her she only cried harder. He apologized again and again for upsetting her. She threw him out of the house.

Their conversation is one for the history books:

"But I am your husband. I am married to you."

"No you're just a monk. You don't know how to love a woman!"

"That's not true. I love all beings."

"Oh, you're dumb! I said you don't know how to love women!"

"I love women too." (*Spring Wind,* p. 31)

Concluding the exchange that started the whole *Men Are From Mars, Women Are From Venus* explanation of male-female relationships, she threw him out and told him he and his two-stone Buddha could live in the shed with the cow.

Pusol was thrilled. He tracked down the stones, cleaned up a corner of the shed, and built a small altar for himself. Meanwhile Wonderful Flower couldn't decide whether she loved or hated him. One moment things were okay, the next moment she was furious that he had left her alone in bed. Real Venus behavior. She started calling him "good for nothing," which Pusol actually enjoyed, figuring that his wife was doing a pretty good job of describing the unobstructed stage of a Bodhisattva.

The couple eventually had two children, a boy named Riding Cloud, and a girl, Bright Moon. After Wonderful Flower's parents died Pusol started to spend more and more time in the cowshed. When he reached his fifties he sat his wife and children down and told them that he had had an attack of paralysis and would have to stay in the shed permanently. Two years later he emerged and started doing chores as though he had never been gone.

Twenty years after leaving their dharma brother, Yongjo and Yonghi showed up one day to see what had happened to Pusol. After meeting his children and spending time with his wife, they begged their friend to join them again.

In reply Pusol asked his children to fill three bottles of water and tie them to the roof beams. He turned to his friends. "Like our Buddha nature, water does not have a fixed form of its own, so water can be contained in many different shapes of vessels but it remains the same in its nature and essence." He asked Yongjo and Yonghi to break their bottles. Picking up sticks, they whacked the bottles, breaking them. Water spilled everywhere. Then Pusol whacked the third bottle. Instead of spilling, the water stayed in the air, floating where the bottle had been.

Pusol turned to his family and friends. "I just wanted to show you that bottles can be broken like our physical body but water remains free from destruction. It is the same with our Buddha mind. Our Buddha mind is free and not subject to the cycle of birth and death because it is our own unborn mind." Looking at him, everyone else suddenly realized that he was truly awakened. Pusol asked his friends to be there for his children if they were ever in need and asked his son and daughter to follow the monks' guidance when he died, which he predicted would happen very soon. He told them: "Attain enlightenment for the sake of all beings. Do not grieve. I will always be with you in dharma. I will be at your side in difficult times and guide and protect you. Remember what I have said." Then he turned to Wonderful Flower. "I have been happy being with you this while. But like all things in life we must part now." He held her hands and, sure enough, died. She wept for a year. (*Spring Wind*, p. 35)

Okay, I couldn't be Pusol. But Sunim might be my Wonderful Flower, a teaching Buddha! A Bodhisattva shining a light on all my weaknesses in the ten directions. When I was able to think of him in this way it always brought a smile to my face. A well-disguised Buddha.

Then I heard about the burnings, which gave me a whole new point of view as well as a startling definition of resolve.

In the good old days, up until maybe the mid 1990s, one of the ways a monk or nun demonstrated his or her sincerity in following the foot-steps of the Buddha was to burn off their fingers, starting with the fourth digit of the left hand, then the last finger of the left hand, then the fourth finger on the right, etc. The original purpose of the burnings was to decrease the choices in livelihood open to the monk or nun. For exam-ple, if you had no trigger finger you could not be a member of the armed forces or hunt. If you couldn't hold a pen you couldn't write. Plus the missing digits offered an instant indicator of someone's determination to become fully enlightened in this lifetime.

(You might want to skip the next few paragraphs if the thought of burning off fingers makes you queasy. I'm about to get graphic.) Basi-cally the young man or woman ties a cord around his/her entire hand above the thumb. This cuts off the blood supply to the fingers and dead-ens the nerves of the hand. Then a candle is melted over a strip of hemp cloth and the resulting waxy material is wrapped around the finger to be sacrificed. Some of the material is left over the top of the finger to serve as a wick which is then lit with a candle. The finger goes up like a torch. As it burns, the young monk or nun usually chants in an effort to sustain his or her total concentration.

I had heard rumors about individual monks and nuns burning their fingers off. Still, it was a total shock to see a completely digit-free hand. It belonged to one of the first Zen masters we visited. A first we were so busy doing prostrations to him and keeping our eyes down that all I noticed were the fancy Zen-related etchings that covered the thick yel-low plastic *ondol* floor. When I couldn't stand looking down any more and curiosity got the best of me (or after about five minutes) I started to take in the rest of the room. Directly across from us was a huge painting on the wall. No. It was actually calligraphy that mapped out the shape of Quanseum Posal (the bodhisattva of compassion) where each mark on the paper was a character in a sutra. Very clever. There were statues everywhere, handcrafted furniture, books, gifts from students, plants, and behind a large low writing desk, Iltal. At first only his head and shoulders were in my line of sight. Then he waved his hand toward a bunch of huge purple grapes that had been set on the floor in front of us. My eyes stopped right there. His hand had no fingers. Only a thumb. Unimaginable. Yet, there it was. He had been determined to ensure that he would never return to lay life and it had worked. It made thinking of Sunim as Wonderful Flower Buddha no big deal somehow. It wasn't like we were headed somewhere to burn off our fingers.

And sometimes there were hilarious moments that dove at us out of nowhere, making the pilgrimage less grim. Many happened in tearooms. Like the time Sunim told us the story of Vagina Valley with a completely straight face. During the reign of Queen Sondok, over a thousand years ago, hundreds of frogs suddenly started croaking in the dead of winter. Upon hearing them, the queen told her two top generals to take two thousand of their best soldiers and go defeat the hidden enemy troops they would find in Vagina Valley. Off they went, surprising five hundred troops who were right where the queen said they would be, as well as another thirteen hundred troops they found hidden behind rocks above the valley. After returning home, one of the generals asked the queen how she knew they were there. She replied that the frogs were croaking away in Vulva Lake, which symbolizes yin, and which symbolizes west. She knew the soldiers were there. "And since a penis always shrinks in a vulva I figured the enemy would be easily defeated." And they were. I swear not once did Sunim crack a smile while we wrote notes.

If there is any Zen significance to the story I haven't found it.

HOW TO SPEND THREE HOURS
IN A TEAROOM

1. Drink pine needle tea, one cup. Drink it slowly because it is very, very sweet and a little bit alcoholic.

2. Eat one of the teeny cookies the tearoom owner puts in front of you so you won't insult her. Don't show your surprise that it isn't sweet.

3. Drink a cup of green tea.

4. Eat a *tok*, a square of cooked sticky rice that is colored green.

5. Drink another cup of green tea. Be glad the cups are slightly larger than thimbles.

6. Eat an apple slice and one half of a green tea cookie, a delicacy sent to the tearoom owner by her sister.

7. Listen to the sweet Korean love song on the CD playing in the background.

8. Drink another cup of green tea.

9. Look at the pictures on the wall. Ask about them because each one has a wonderful story.

10. Write in your journal. Try some haiku. Rip it up before anyone tries to read it over your shoulder.

11. Sing songs out loud. Lullabies are good. Or you can take a catnap. No one will notice because they are all taking their own catnaps.

12. Go to the rest room.

13. Take a quick walk in the rain for some fresh air.

14. Look at the pictures in the Korean books beside the table.

15. Drink a cup of green tea, this time from the special collection of the tea shop owner.

16. Sign the guest book. Feel honored because not everyone is invited to sign it. Write a poem in it if you can think of one.

17. Practice writing Korean letters.

18. Look at some more pictures.

19. Since by now you will be in love with both the tearoom and its owner, take photos.

20. Say thank you and leave.

Chapter Seven

Just This

MEDITATION

A hundred hammers on my head
and I'm still not awake.

All morning the bees drone.
I slap them away.

No one dares come close.
I am too full of myself,
stuffed and drowsy

struggling up the trail
hoping to escape
the hands of those who love me,

hoping to arrive
alone there

the summit—
one crooked pine
wind beaten
holding on,

how we must all look
climbing up this mountain,
shaved heads, itchy with stubble,
faces brown, hardened

and the grit between our teeth
settling in.

Sue Budin
Dharma sister
Ann Arbor, Michigan
February, 2000

Journal entry: August 31, 1999, Taegu

"Every day at 4 A.M. in a tiny city in the middle of these mountains two young monks and ten elderly women chant for the peace and happiness of the whole world for one and a half hours. We got up to join them today. Chanting, chanting, chanting. More than an hour. One hundred and twenty prostrations to go with it. Yesterday we were up at 3 A.M. for prostrations and *Yebul*. Then back to sit in our room after a lecture on Buddhist practices. A hot (sort of) shower. Basically you put hot water in a big bowl and then with a scoop throw it all over yourself. Fun. Breakfast: rice, veggies (unrecognizable—maybe roots?), kimchi. So many bodhisattvas are coming out of the woodwork to help us. A monk thrust his own umbrella at us when we left. Insisted we take it. Waved us away in the downpour."

When you are travelling with a Zen master who studied at Pomosa, you visit Pomosa. The name of the temple comes from a famous legend about a well that was filled with golden-hued water. Word was the water had special magical properties, and the fish who swam in the water were believed to have come directly from Nirvana, the state of nonsuffering. So Pomosa literally means "where fish from Nirvana play."

Samu Sunim went to Pomosa in the spring of 1962, by way of the long-winding mountain road that ends at its gates. At the time some two hundred monks and nuns were living in the compound's nine subtemples and hermitages. There Sunim became a disciple of Tongsan Sunim (1890–1965), the spiritual head of the monastic community. Tongsan had been the supreme patriarch of the Chogye order prior to that time. In other words, he was a very big deal. According to Sunim, Tongsan Sunim scrupulously adhered to the precepts and pure rules of a monastic community during his tenure as head monk, constantly urging the monks to penetrate the *hwadu*, "Where am I at the moment where there is neither a dream or a thought?"

Sunim was also a student of Pomosa's Solbong Sunim (1890–1969), who "resembled an old tiger crouched in his cave." Solbong Sunim was quite the character, known for drinking, sleeping on the streets, and "mingling freely with ordinary folks." Every once in a while he would disappear from the monastery to spend time with his worldly friends at the bottom of the mountain, later resurfacing to give powerful dharma talks to the monks: "To free oneself from worldly possessions is a difficult thing for an ordinary being to do. More difficult still is to give oneself totally, body and mind, after the renunciation. If you lack an earnest mind it is difficult to let go of yourself. Without letting go of yourself completely you will not be able to break through." (Zen Lotus Society Handbook, p. 19)

Pomosa is perched on one of Korea's favorite mountains for hikers and naturalists, Mt. Kumjung. Even when the temple is closed to outsiders people have a way of sneaking in. Often what gives them the courage to break into such a place is the alcohol they've just consumed. Established in 678, the monastery has been home to many a young monk or nun seeking enlightenment. Recently renovated, the temple is well known for its ancient stone pagodas and lanterns, as well as its eccentric Zen masters. In addition to Solbong Sunim, one of Samu Sunim's favorites was the small, stout Ho Sunim. He was known for strolling the temple grounds bare chested, even in the dead of winter. He constantly fanned himself, year round, with an old-fashioned rigid Korean fan which had five characters written on it: Fresh wind arises with every step. It was apparently quite a sight to see him walking around in gray baggy pants, bare chested, fanning himself.

Ho Sunim made it his job to patrol the temple grounds for unauthorized intruders. He used to walk around unnoticed, until he spotted someone crawling under a fence into the temple, or urinating somewhere out in the open. He would walk up behind them and then bellow, "You thief!" After jumping out of their shoes, most people would yell back that they weren't thieves—that they hadn't stolen anything! To which Ho

Sunim would respond with something like, "If you're not a thief, why are you crawling under someone's fence instead of coming onto the grounds through the gate? If you still think you aren't a thief then apologize for trespassing!" If the person immediately apologized, Ho Sunim would look him right in the eye and say, "You're a superior person. You will become a Buddha without fail." If the person hesitated or refused to apologize, Ho Sunim would shout at them, "You're impossible! Go away!" My guess is that single encounter was enough to stop anyone from breaking into any other temple probably forever.

You can feel the energy of Ho Sunim and Solbong Sunim and all of their ancestors as you walk through the grounds. More compact than the huge compounds of Heinsa and Tongdosa, Pomosa is a nook and cranny temple with lots of corners and surprise plazas, tiny gardens popping out of nowhere, and a constant stream of visitors.

I was completely excited about travelling to Pomosa. I was hungry to see where my teacher had studied, what the rooms were like, especially his. I wanted to smell the smells he had smelled and to see the scenes he had seen. But we were tired when we arrived and it was raining hard. None of the "old timers" knew Sunim, so we were treated with a perfunctory courtesy that didn't go over too well. I watched Sunim's face as it became clear that we were considered tourists in his old home. At first there weren't any clues that he might be upset. There wasn't any yelling or any shouted orders at me and Haju who, by midafternoon, were pretty soaked and scraggly. We spent hours sitting with a university student group on a day retreat while we waited for rooms.

When we finally got them, two on the end of an old building tucked away in the corner of the temple compound, things continued on a downward spiral. The doors didn't close and Sunim's room leaked. A big leak.

There was a short visit with the abbot that evolved into a conversation about how to run successful temples. The abbot had been running the temple for quite a while and was reputed to be one of the most effective administrators in the country. We asked him what he had learned about running a successful temple, one that lasts through time. His answer had three parts. First, he said, it is critical to always put yourself in the place of the members of the community. You need to see the organization or institution through their eyes, experience it from their viewpoint. When you do, many potential problems become clear that you never would have seen from your own position.

The second factor? Patience. In every aspect of running a temple, patience matters. Patience with how long it takes for the new monks to learn the rituals, patience with the posalnims who come to help, patience with the Western women who show up on your doorstep smelly and full of questions. The third piece of advice? Wait and see. We need to wait and see the impact of even the small changes before we take the next step, make the next move. Too often we make decisions when our notions are just plain wrong because all the votes aren't in. I sat there wondering what he would think of e-commerce.

He reminded us to remember to always pay attention to the precepts: not to lie, kill, steal, muddy our minds with drugs or alcohol, not to be sexually promiscuous. Then he gave us some surprise advice. Because our surroundings really, really matter, promoting beauty and providing it as much as possible leads to more harmonious behavior. I think the man could write an entire book on the subject. He made me want to look at where I live and work in a whole different way after I got home. Maybe Martha Stewart is right about all the details and colors and the rest of it. The abbot was pretty convincing. According to him, we should make inner-city schools the most beautiful in the community. We should fill them with flowers and maybe waterfalls.

Since we were sitting on comfortable couches—a rare treat—I wanted to ask for more.

"What else?"

"That's all."

The abbot just smiled and continued to sit with us quietly while I categorized all the major mistakes of my life to see if his paradigm worked in reverse. It did. Either I was way too far over in the land of "me," or I was impatient with the person and situation, or I just didn't have it in me to wait and see. Oh well.

We remained with the abbot about a half hour longer until there was a shout: "Let's go!" So we left. Just like that. Out into the pouring rain of the late afternoon storm. We hitched a ride in one of the university student's vans. Sunim was quiet. Haju and Kaeo slept. I fretted.

∗ ∗ ∗

By the time the pilgrimage was half over it was clear that all the survival mechanisms I thought would work weren't going to be any help. "Just do it" was no match for the utter lack of trail markers, the absence of anything familiar, and an agonizing homesickness worthy of the Waltons.

And yet...

We were surrounded by the most extraordinary compassion from the fervent young monks we met in the mountains and from the old, old women who insisted on giving us fruit and vinegar tea (almost as good as lemonade) for energy. Their acts of kindness kept me going. There was also some part of me determined to understand from my own experience how complete misery could turn into enlightenment or at least a heart of gratitude. After what felt like years had past, finally subtle shifts happened as I began to consciously experience each moment. There was more peacefulness in every situation; more patience; more energy. I still reacted to Sunim's anger, but my reactions didn't last as long. I was still resisting, but not as ferociously or for as long.

Sunim had shrugged off our treatment at Pomosa. Amazingly there were no recriminations about how we were treated, no complaints about the rooms, no debriefings. We just took the next step toward the next place we were to visit.

A new world view began to take hold of my brain: that any situation was survivable if I stayed right smack in the middle of it, letting everything else go. And every day provided ample opportunities to practice being in the middle of situations. On a bus to the city of Taegu, I vaguely remembered a dharma talk (or maybe it was an essay) by a wonderful teacher, Joan Halifax, that described enlightenment as the capacity to really be with both suffering and joy, directly and in an unmediated way. That was the job at hand—to simply be with the suffering and the joy. When we had to wait here or there for Sunim, I just waited: sometimes for minutes, sometimes for hours. Sometimes long enough to memorize the exact position of each pebble on the ground in front of my feet. "Just this, just this, just this," became my mantra, the only thinking allowed.

Staying with whatever was happening "right now" made each experience deeper and sweeter. Trees, plants, stoves, rocks, buildings, and people started to take on auras: halos of soft color. Smells were stronger. I even sensed different vibrations in different places and different vibrations inside of me. Sometimes my whole inside was downright buzzy. "Just this" softened the homesickness over time. It protected what little patience was left hiding in the cells of my exhausted body.

The biggest tests to "just this" practice became what I call "after the fact" teachings. It was *after* I hand washed my clothes with a bar of hand soap, knowing it meant a probable skin rash as a result of what happens when dirt, sweat, heat, rain, cotton, and hand soap collide, that Haju handed me a different bar, saying, "This is the washing soap." Just this, just this, just this, just this. It was *after* I had welts the size of boils all over my arms, legs, and neck from spending the night sharing a room with biting ants I never even knew existed, Sunim told me, "You should have washed the floor." Just this, just this, just this, just this, just this. I think I earned extra bonus points since every inch of my body itched.

The benefits of "just this" practice were enormous. Many things stopped mattering when my mind stopped being locked into them, when my obsessive thinking engine ran out of fuel. Missed meals? No problem. Missed sleep? No problem. Pouring rain day after day in ninety-degree heat? No problem. Almost always wet clothing? No problem. Being ignored for hours or a day at a time? No problem. Being singled out by a total jerk of a monk who demanded prostrations all the while belittling your every movement? Okay, there was still work to be done. A jerk is still a jerk.

"Just this" practice became my warrior's shield, preventing negative reactions to difficult situations and taking on a life of its own somehow. I had been mouthing "just this" for weeks, trying to stay totally concentrated on it. Driving out of Pomosa I suddenly noticed that "just this" was cruising along inside me even though I hadn't been thinking it. All there was was "just this" surrounded by something that felt like a pool of enormous quiet spaciousness.

At first I chalked up these sensations as connected to the hallucinations associated with deprivation. Anyone going so long without cheese, pizza, and National Public Radio (Oh God, where are you Todd Mundt?) was bound to experience strange things.

Except the spaciousness stayed day and night. A slow but steady buildup of spiritual energy made each moment brighter somehow. Also lighter. In this spaciousness everything seemed like poetry.

Meanwhile, once-in-many-lifetimes experiences continued to rush at us. In one day we visited two different nunneries:

Journal entry: August 31, 1999, Taegu again

"We climbed the mountain to a nunnery. It is nestled right beside a waterfall and a rushing mountain river. The *samadhi* energy is palpable. We were invited to visit with a nun, ninety-eight years old, who is the most respected nun in Korea. She demanded that we hold her hands as we knelt beside her on her futon. Her attendant told us she was dying, that today could be the last day of her life. Although blind, she had a sure grip, clear mind, commanding voice. When she was told about Haju and me she almost shouted, 'Thank you! Dharma!' It was so moving. I vowed to keep going, to go deeper, to not let anything into my brain but practice. We toured the compound surrounded by the sound of rushing water, the clear air, and the nun's pure energy.

"From there, we walked to a second nunnery where a young nun served us diluted coffee and fruit. She served us as though we were the lost kings and queens she had been waiting for all her life. Every movement was ballet. As I watched her silhouetted against the mountains behind her, I told myself to slow down the next time I served anyone diluted coffee and fruit. Go for the ballet."

Compassion popped up from behind bushes and rocks and buildings. Dainin Katagiri once said that compassion "is like spring water under the ground. Your life is like a pipe that can tap into that underground spring. When you tap into it, water immediately comes up. So drive your pipe into the ground. Tap into the water of compassion. We can't conceive of what real compassion and openness of heart are, but if you tap into them, you can feel them. If you learn to deal with your life with compassion, magnanimity, and flexibility, you will become very tender, generous, and kind. This is all that is necessary." ("Opening Your Heart," *Shambala Sun*, September, 1999, p. 43)

Kindness was everywhere, it seemed. We arrived long after dark at a city monastery on the southern tip of the peninsula. We were met by an elderly man, Mr. Yang, who hovered around us until he was sure we had each found our rooms, the bathrooms, and the washroom. He couldn't do enough for us. In the morning, sensing how exhausted we were, he made cups of coffee for us at breakfast. Then he took us on a tour of a kindergarten that is connected to the temple. The headmaster, determined that ancient Korean culture thrive in a world drowning in cybertechnology, has created a miniature Korean version of Disneyworld for the children. They learn how to drum and make music on ancient instruments. There is also a garden of indigenous grains that are cultivated and then harvested and made into flour in a miniature mill where the students can actually learn how to use the old tools so they can harvest the grain themselves. Surrounded by buildings made of clay, in a playground of ancient machines, kindness was everywhere.

When we left our wonderful caretaker insisted on carrying four of our backpacks (by then we each had at least two, mostly filled with books) to where we were to get a ride to the bus station and handed each of us envelopes with money in them. It was probably all the money he had, certainly more than a month's wages.

I was constantly moved by the spontaneous acts of kindness shown us by women, even when it meant breaking their own rules of protocol. In a city temple where we appeared without warning one night in the middle of a downpour, the kitchen women grabbed Haju's and my hands and pulled us through the kitchen to a teeny bathroom, no more than three feet by three feet. There, one of the younger women showed us how to hook a piece of hose onto the sink for a makeshift shower, knowing we weren't supposed to wash for days yet. It was after 10 P.M. lights out and we were all supposed to be in bed. No matter. Happy to strip I stepped into the makeshift shower as quietly as I could, rigged up the hose, and turned on the faucet. Heaven. Suddenly a fist appeared at shoulder level. It opened. Four tiny bottles were in it: shampoo, cream rinse, body lotion, perfume. Having never shampooed a bald head I had the time of my life lathering up. A solid rinsing later, there was a knock.

A cake of soap appeared for me to use to wash my socks which were standing upright in their own filth. As we snuck back to our room, that a small office beside the main dining hall, another woman scurried around trying to catch a cockroach so we wouldn't be disturbed by its night ramblings. Then she opened a little window for us to get some fresh air. Sunim, of course, inevitably yelled at us to close it, but for a short while it was nice to lie on the floor, luxuriously clean, listening to the rain.

For weeks rain poured down as though the sky's heart was broken. Thunder turned the heavens into a master level bowling league. It definitely slowed us down, but it also made it possible to be further spoiled by more acts of kindness. Some even came from Sunim. The treat of a Korean massage made bygones bygones, rubbing our karmic slate clean.

* * *

HOW TO GET A KOREAN MASSAGE

First find a bathhouse. Then pay the young woman at the counter about $1.50 for a bath. You'll be given a key which opens a door into what looks like someone's living room except that there are lockers behind the couches and two middle-aged women walking around in black lace bras and underpants. Try not to stare. Strip. Look to your left. Through the doorway you will see a lineup of naked women—all shapes, sizes, and ages. Each one is sitting on a child's stool in front of a bucket of water and a faucet. Join them. They'll show you how to use the bar of soap next to your selected faucet to lather up. Lather up. Rinse. Lather up. Rinse. Try not to look at your rinse water which is a sort of iridescent gray green. Try not to wonder what the green part is all about. Try not to think that you have just discovered a perfect car color shade for the next—hopefully more ecologically sensitive—four-wheel-drive you've decided you need back home.

Then hit the sauna. After ten minutes leave the sauna room to pour cold water all over yourself from the miniature blue tile swimming pool in the middle of the room. Go back into the sauna to sit for about fifteen minutes with the half dozen women watching soap operas on a TV set sitting on the sauna room floor. Another rinse, only this time in a tiled Jacuzzi next to the sauna.

Now for the good part. Walk around the paneled wall at the back of the main room. There you'll see a huge silver metal table, maybe eight feet long and three feet wide, next to a waist-high trough of water. One of the black lace bra ladies will motion to you to climb onto the table which, if you are under five feet five inches, will be a little high. It will also be very slippery because of the water splashing onto it from trough overflow. The sensation of climbing up onto it will bring back instant memories of trying to climb back up metal playground slides when you were little. If you stay put in the memory you'll even remember what they tasted like.

Try not to slide right past the woman (who is now standing at one end of the table) and into the trough. This takes concentration and a firm grasp of the table's edges.

Lie on your back on the table. The woman will immediately cover your face with cucumber mush so you won't be able to see what she is about to do, which is to scrub (with all her formidable strength) your body clean from head to toe and back again with what feels suspiciously like a pot scrubber. If you don't scream out "Stop! I beg you, stop!" because your "just this" practice is actually working, you will end up cleaner than you've ever been in your life. Your skin will be as soft as it was twenty, no thirty, years ago. It will actually glow. If you smile a lot while all this is being done, the woman will give you an ice-cold Coca Cola in a can as a reward for your good behavior. Even if it is 5 A.M.

* * *

Journal entry: September 1, 1999, Pulguksa

"'Just this' mind really works! It is shifting into 'don't know' mind. When there is no mind, there are no problems. Everywhere and everything is just fine. Which doesn't mean that you don't work with what's in front of you. It's just that that's all you do. I'm irritated that I've let Bill B. and all his stuff follow me all the way to Korea—although here I see him as a genuine Bodhisattva. (I paid him all the money I had to build a road on a piece of property I wanted to use for a retreat center. He drank it.) His behavior forced me to make decisions I didn't want to make. Here, beside this road in the middle of somewhere, I realize that the universe will give me a place if I'm to start a temple. And that is that."

By the middle of the pilgrimage we were climbing more, our practice constant. To stay up all night was no longer the exception, especially if there were biting insects in our room. Five-mile hikes with more than a mile straight up the sides of mountains took us to amazing spots—sometimes with huge stone Buddhas carved right into the rocks. At one point we climbed until we reached a three-foot ledge where Wonhyo, hero of heroes, Korea's first rock'n'roll monk, used to spend the night. Reaching the ledge I kept thinking about Wonhyo's genius, his insistence that enlightenment is within reach of all comers: "One who isn't restricted to everyday affairs, with a single mind frees himself from birth and death. He is a friend of rocks, trees, and clouds." We were looking straight down over the clouds and could see all of Kyongjin, an ancient city. The mountains looked like a lumpy quilt covering the earth.

Climbing back down the mountain brought us back into the realm of compassion. We stopped at a small hermitage, unannounced. Within seconds of Sunim's yelling, "Your guests are here!" A nun came out, invited us inside and fed us bananas (an unexpected treat) and a sparkly juice. She also gave Sunim some travelling money for us. Only hours later we accidentally met up with two monks Sunim had known years ago. One insisted that we join him for lunch. I counted eighteen different types of food in the serving dishes that completely covered two tables where we sat.

* * *

It was really something to be the only two women surrounded by monks most of the time. Their kindness was deep. In the meditation halls they chanted sutras for the sake of all beings, sounding like a men's choral group on a world tour. The sound was intense and moving. And not once were we silenced when Haju and I added our wobbly female voices to the sound, throwing it way off center. She knew the words and I knew the tune. The sum of our voices, however, was far less than each part. We pretty much sucked.

When we visited individual monks in their own small hermitages they burst with generosity. Suan Sunim is a famous Korean artist and poet, best known for his "Innocent Gestures" paintings. One of his most recognizable designs is a picture, almost a line drawing, of a simple clay bowl with the sun rising behind it. When we showed up for a visit, I asked him about the drawing. He explained that the bowl contains the whole universe: rain, snow, happiness, sadness. The sun shines on all of it. Suan Sunim first entered a monastery as a carpenter and met Samu Sunim when they were both young. After many years in a monastic setting, he headed out on his own. His art became his practice. When we showed up for a visit, some thirty-plus years later, Suan Sunim plied us with gifts of books, postcards, tea towels, and envelopes of money. Later, another monk who runs a compassion house for orphans insisted that we share some of his very expensive Chinese tea. At $1,000 for a small jar of the tea leaves, we drank each cup slowly. After about ten cups each, he finally allowed us to politely refuse another cup. As far as he was concerned it would have been just fine if we had consumed the entire jar—his only asset as far as I could tell.

Most amazingly, the monks taught me love. How bizarre is that?! It was completely strange, at first, to spend so much time with men who aren't obsessed or, for the most part, even interested in sex, power, or money. Everywhere we went the monks were giving us food, books, keepsakes, and money. Sometimes it felt like they were giving us most of what they had. Never once did I see a girly picture or hear a sexual comment about women or other men. In contrast, how many conversations do most of us have where there isn't at least something that could stray into the realm of sexual innuendo given half the chance? As for power, it seemed like the real struggle in the monasteries was to get the monks to accept power rather than having factions fighting for control. (Okay, there were a couple of exceptions but they were rare.)

My first experience of what truly loving someone is all about happened in Seoul when one of the young monks silently put a bag of M&Ms (Korea's version) into my hand before we left for the mountains. He knew what we were getting into and guessed what I would yearn for on the worst day. All this with not a word spoken. Another young monk (maybe he was eighteen years old) insisted on serving me his best green tea. When I glanced into the eyes of each of these young men before bowing in gratitude, all I saw was love. It was love like the love in your first boyfriend's eyes when he just can't hide the fact that he's head over heels and will do anything for you. That love. At first, I figured I was hallucinating or having some form of psychic withdrawal like when I tried to give up chocolate and kept seeing it everywhere I looked, including my dreams.

Except it kept happening. Like the time a young artist monk was looking straight through me as though we had just made love and were lying together afterwards. And the absolute last thing I imagined I would be seeing were monks so handsome they could model for GQ magazine. Yet in every monastery there were at least a handful who could have given Justin Timberlake, Tom Cruise, and yes, even Richard Gere a run for their money. One was the most beautiful man I have ever seen in my life—a deer reborn as a person with huge black clear eyes, swarthy skin, the perfect Pepsodent smile. Tall, thin. Disconcerting.

The younger monks would often wave at us and grin from a distance. When we were staying at their temples, they smiled at all our mistakes and awkwardness. Sometimes they smiled in encouragement as though we were best friends. It felt like they would help us in any way they knew how. At the highest Chiri mountain hermitage, we showed up just as six young monks decided to continue their intensive summer retreat past its formal finish. One of them came down the path to greet us. He looked like a cross between Jeff Goldblum and Andy Garcia. He took our bags and carried them up the last part of the trail. At the top, everyone else got their bags back. But he held onto mine, and smiling, he walked me to a tiny room on the corner of one of the hermitage's buildings. It was a monk's room, maybe six feet square, empty except for a small dresser and tea set. Putting the bags just inside the door he smiled at me again, leaving me breathless. And feeling stupid. What was this rush of emotion? His eyes were clear, and completely accepting of everything in sight including me. He was completely judgment and expectation free. The whole time we were at the hermitage he cared for us. He was like a guardian angel shadow, making sure everything was okay. Fruit and cookies slipped into our room that night. In the morning two tiny cartons of real milk appeared—no small task given that everything had to be hand carted all the way up the mountain. All this without words. I knew that if I decided to stay it would be just fine with him, and if I left it would be just fine. It wouldn't change the love.

When we left, the same smile, the "Where you are, I am too" smile. A flash of "Dear God, could I please oh please have a monk?" on my part (okay, okay habits die hard. This is not about sainthood). Then one more smile and the climb back down the mountain. Even now, thinking about the monks reminds me of the endless possibilities in relationships built on compassion and love without expectation.

The young monks' single-minded determination to protect the dharma was something to see and experience first hand. It taught me so much about the capacity of the human heart—and showed me that we really can completely dedicate ourselves to compassion and kindness, and thrive. Their determination called me on my biases about the generations growing up behind us. There are warriors there—young people willing to dedicate their whole lives to making ours better. I could not have imagined that young men and women would willingly cloister themselves for months and months simply to chant and meditate for the sake of all beings. If I hadn't seen it with my own eyes I can't say I would have believed someone else describing their efforts. No way, I would have thought. Too hard.

But there they were.

Monks who vowed not to leave a temple until they were enlightened, practicing in absolute silence, only eating once a day, never lying down. Whew. We were so high in the mountains, within touch of the clouds, that it was easy to feel how the sky would protect their tenaciousness.

Zen Master Taeil Sunim was the one who set the standards. Seventy years old, he was a "simple country boy" who literally built a mountain temple with his bare hands. To buy materials he saved travelling money given to him by other monks. His first purchase was tin, to build an outhouse. When it was finished he climbed down his mountain to raise more money only to find the outhouse destroyed on his return. So he rebuilt it. Next trip, torn down again. Rebuilt. Torn down. Finally, Taeil Sunim hired a local worker, a man with four small boys whose wife had run away, to help him rebuild the outhouse and protect the property. Instead the man hanged himself, leaving behind four orphans. The two youngest boys, five and six years old respectively, were taken in by Taeil Sunim.

Meanwhile a local woman, whose husband had lost his eyesight in an explosion at his factory, decided there must be someone in the mountains who could help her husband (rumors of miracle healings by the monks are pretty common. I didn't see any. Oh well). She literally carried her husband up the mountain to where Taeil Sunim was staying with the two young boys. Taeil offered his room to her husband. Four times a day the husband would crawl to the altar to do chanting practice. The woman became the temple's cook. Concerned about the corruption of the outside world, Taeil made a vow to build his temple without electricity, a road, or telephones. (I'm guessing he's never seen a computer.) He hired local women to carry wood on their heads up the mountain. Slowly but surely the temple was built.

When the woman's husband died, she stayed. The boys are now men and Taeil Sunim is the father some of us wish we had.

After visiting Taeil Sunim, I knew I would see the pilgrimage through. His quiet charm and never-ending humor in the face of years and years of hardship were a reminder of the benefits of sustained practice in the face of whatever life decides to throw our way. He had been through so much and there he was, an old man, folding his legs up like an origami bird so he could sit at a table a foot off the ground, watching to make sure all of his orphans, us included, had enough food, enough tea, making treats appear like magic, sweet rice balls and cakes, so every meal felt like a party. Cracking jokes right and left. Maybe tomorrow everything would be gone. His young monks might defect to the city. The temple posalnims might leave for America. No matter. He would just keep feeding everyone rice treats and living life lightly.

Watching his wide openhearted approach to his own life, I knew I could keep going. I could keep going because I was seeing the long-term benefits of sincere spiritual practice everywhere we went. An open-armed acceptance of life. Clarity and contentedness. Sheer happiness. Giggles. It was in the monks and nuns and many of the posalnims living at the temples. An "okayness" with everything. It beat any drug-induced, caffeine-driven morning-after euphoria I had ever known. Sheer happiness smack in the middle of ordinary life. Taeil Sunim glowed with it and so did everyone around him. And Sunim was doing his best to show us how to get there from here.

A new source of energy sprouted up from nowhere. Sitting at Taeil Sunim's breakfast table, my body actually jolted. I looked up to see if anyone noticed. Taeil Sunim, sitting across from me at the next low table, was watching me, smiling.

Maybe I'd never be Pusol, ever, and the monks' compassion would leave this puppy in the dirt in any race toward Bodhisattvahood, but I could be the best me and see where that lead. The mountains held us up and the sky was a perfect shelter. And it didn't hurt to feel that the bag of M&Ms was still unopened in my pocket.

Chapter Eight

Climbing Mountains in Typhoons Practice

MOUNTAIN DHARMA

Mist rises
and the pines
   the rocks below
   wake up
as if inside them
there were no hearts beating—
no sound
but a shimmering,
the green having taken on
its greenness

and the lichened rock
hunched like this monk.
Brown-robed he comes
to sit here,
spends mornings with the sun
who dries the hollow
in that rock
where he rests.

The holy man can hear
not with his ears
but heart,
the heart inside the rock
speaking
maybe singing
maybe chanting
maybe only one sound
like a folded wing
opening and closing.

Sue Budin
Dharma sister
Ann Arbor, Michigan
February, 2000

Journal entry: September 8, 1999, Yongwonsa

"Just went over Chiri Mountain after visiting Ssanggesa. We hiked three miles. Half straight up and half straight down. Then, because of the rain, we got a ride over the mountains instead of making our way by foot through the pass. Sunim kept saying, 'This is the last mountain.' It never was. Last night, suddenly back plotting my way home, after I had been so sure of finishing this trip only hours earlier. What a frigging roller coaster ride. I actually lay awake figuring it out. I guess these 3 A.M. arisings combined with evening sittings that go on and on (I just got up and left last night) have me more frazzled than I thought. But I slept a little extra this morning while Haju sat…and a dream later, feel better. Now sitting in front of a little 'everything' store. Sunim and Kaeo are off somewhere. As they walked off Sunim looked back at me: 'Don't run away.' I'm tired of that man reading my mind.

"We're waiting for a bus (I don't know the number) to go to a temple (don't know which one…we're way past anything you can find on maps). Hilarious."

* * *

Ssanggesa Temple: No memory. No notes. My exhaustion was so deep by then that most of my time was spent perfecting the fine art of sleeping in any posture: standing, walking, seated, or lying down. A useful skill I continue to use today. A skill I learned in the heat, the rain, and the mountains, should you have a problem falling asleep and be looking for a solution. I think one of the monks we talked to told us the key to enlightenment but I can't remember if he said it was feetless or fearless. See what I mean about the exhaustion part?

There is a barely legible line in my journal that says, "The head of Hui-neng, the 6th Patriarch, is believed to be in Ssanggesa." That just may be. There seems to be quite a fascination with the different uses for body parts in this tradition. We're not alone apparently. A recent article in

Mandala magazine told the story of a man named Noberto Manero who served twelve years in prison in the Philippines for murdering and then eating a Catholic priest. According to the article, prison seems to have had quite a positive impact on him. "I no longer have a taste for men of the cloth… I eat only cabbage and lentils. During my time in prison I converted to Islam and became a vegetarian, so it would be strictly against my beliefs to eat anyone at all."

He is planning to open a restaurant with his brothers in the north where there are few priests so he "won't be tempted." His words. Makes a stupa around Hui-neng's head no big deal somehow. (*Mandala*, May-June, 2000, p. 6)

* * *

Just when it felt like things would work out, everything got harder. Suddenly we weren't climbing mountains in rainstorms, we were climbing them in a typhoon so strong it was reported on CNN News for a week. We were drenched by a combination of rain and sweat, sometimes getting mired in places where it was unclear whether we would get out. Facing death became a factor in the pilgrimage, for extra karmic bonus points I guess. Twice I actually mentally said goodbye to my family and friends, telling them how much I loved them before we fell to a certain death. There was only one way out of the muck. To just trust that somehow we would make it.

I would just stick with "don't know" mind, literally living moment to moment and leave the rest to Buddha. I found myself clinging to particular teachings that I started calling "The Survival Sutras." One was the Satipatthana Sutra, a teaching on the four foundations of mindfulness that promises simple awareness can get anybody through anything: "On whatever occasion a monk trains himself to breathe in…and…out calming mental processes…" It even promises that such awareness, however it is triggered, will naturally evolve into awakening:

1. On whatever occasion the monk remains focused on the body in and of itself—ardent, aware, and mindful—subduing greed and sorrow with reference to the world, on that occasion his mindfulness is ready and without lapse. When his mindfulness is ready and without lapse, then mindfulness as a factor of awakening becomes aroused, he develops it and through development it comes to completion.

2. Remaining mindful in this way, he examines, analyzes, and comes to a comprehension of that phenomenon with discernment. When he remains mindful in this way, examining, analyzing, and coming to a comprehension of that phenomenon with discernment, then investigation of phenomena as a factor of awakening becomes aroused, he develops it and through development it comes to completion.

3. In one who examines, analyzes, and comes to a comprehension of that phenomena with discernment, unflagging persistence is aroused. When unflagging persistence is aroused in one who examines, analyzes, and comes to a comprehension of that phenomenon with discernment, then persistence as a factor of awakening becomes aroused, he develops it and through development it comes to completion.

4. In one whose persistence is aroused, a rapture not-of-the-flesh arises. When a rapture not-of-the-flesh arises in one whose persistence is aroused, then rapture as a factor of awakening becomes aroused, he develops it and through development it comes to completion.

5. For one who is enraptured, the body grows calm and the mind grows calm. When the body and mind of an enraptured monk become calm, then tranquility as a factor of awakening becomes aroused, he develops it and through development it comes to completion.

6. For one who is at ease—his body calmed—the mind becomes concentrated. When the mind of one who is at ease—his body calmed—

becomes concentrated, then concentration as a factor of awakening becomes aroused, he develops it and through development it comes to completion.

7. He oversees the mind thus concentrated with complete equanimity. When he oversees the mind thus concentrated with complete equanimity, equanimity as a factor of awakening becomes aroused, he develops it and through development it comes to completion. (A fuller translation by Thanissaro Bikkhu can be found at www.saigon.com/~hoasen/4foundat.htm)

Sort of gave me something to shoot for.

The combination of rain and wind, sleepless nights, constant movement from temple to temple with backpacks filled with Sunim's books, and an absence of protein meant that only the primal parts of each of us were operating by this point. Every experience was surrounded by a cloud of bone tiredness. Plus, the farther into the mountains we went the more obstacles we faced. Like poisonous snakes and washed out roads, falling rocks, and signless paths.

On top of everything else we really smelled. Stank. At least I did. In public places people started holding their noses as we approached. When we were lucky enough to travel from one city to the next by train people got up and moved to different seats the way we do here when a homeless person smelling of alcohol joins our ranks. As we waited for buses people moved away from us. Young girls pulled out handkerchiefs to delicately cover their noses. Men put newspapers over their noses and mouths. There was nothing to do but watch their reactions with a growing feeling that I was getting a first taste of something akin to racism, and it wasn't pleasant.

Thankfully there were moments of great humor. The sudden realization that I would have shaved my head, even if I had come with hair, just to get through the trip. So all my bracing of self for the experience of no hair, using the shaving as proof of my sincere willingness to be a model follower of the way, was for nothing. This was a practical matter. Sitting in our second, and last, bathhouse at 7 A.M. on a Sunday in a small southern city surrounded by naked Korean women who didn't speak a word of English, having finally mastered only two expressions in Korean, "thank you" and "hurry up," I suddenly noticed that I knew the words to every song being played over the building-wide intercom system. The Beatles. Chicago's "If you leave me now, you'll take away the biggest ("biggest" was the word wasn't it?) part of me... Ooooooh baby please don't go."

* * *

I started listing the lessons I was learning on little scraps of paper whenever they popped up, tucking them into my pockets for later review. Here are some that were still legible when I pulled them out of my pockets:

1. The way to travel with Zen masters is to seize any opportunity offered to:
   A. drink water;
   B. use the toilet; or
   C. mail letters.
   ANSWER: All of the above. All the time. Further commentary: It takes a special form of mindfulness to do this well—a combination of paying attention and trying to guess what they are thinking. You combine these two practices with a calibration of how much time you have before the (train, bus, car) leaves and/or how much time you have before the scoldings start and you're off...

2. I only need about a fourth of what I own. If we make it back alive I'll have a fire sale.

3. Good food equals good health.

4. I'll never take a toilet seat for granted again. Ever.

5. Heaven is everywhere. Why? Because we carry it with us. (I must have copied that from somewhere else. Sounds too Confucian for this Buddha puppy.)

* * *

Even with distractions Sunim got grouchier and grouchier with time. Corrections increased in number and intensity as we crossed over mountains and half walked, half ran from place to place. Corrections and more corrections. Trying to think ahead to head off mistakes didn't work. Trying to be extra helpful didn't help either. Sunim kept getting grouchier. At one of the poison-snakes-are-everywhere-so-be-careful temples I offered Sunim a flashlight on my way back from the bathroom, so he could see the path. It was pretty darn dark. "Turn that off. You don't need it here." One morning I just cried for two hours straight from the sheer effort of it all. I wasn't really sad, just tired. I finally stopped because my eyes were just about swollen shut.

I lost count of how many temples we had visited. Maybe thirty given that we visited as many as four on some days. Pulguksa. Heinsa. Popchangsa. Tongdosa. Pomosa. Naewonsa. Ssanggesa. Chilbulsa. Yongwonsa. They all merged into a single image of a Buddha hall with at least one huge golden Buddha half smiling at us, eyes down. All the kitchens promised rice, kimchi, vegetables, and tea. All the bedrooms, furniture-free floors for sleeping, a futon if we were lucky, a tiny window if we were really really lucky.

My sneakers, white Keds, were pretty much shot. The lining had literally crumbled into nothing until there was no lining so I was hiking on a thin slab of canvas. As if to help me ignore the discomfort, every mountain path offered something beautiful. We, however, were far from beautiful. Everywhere people stared at the motley group we had become. Smelly. Dirty. Patched. Bald. Lugging backpacks and big plastic bags of books. Even the monks stared.

* * *

Deciding that "just this" wasn't getting me through the pilgrimage without flashes of anger, resentment, and self-pity, I looked for additional guidelines. We arrived at Hwaomsa Temple in the nick of time. It was filled with guidelines and grace.

One of the sutras or teachings that has greatly influenced Korean Buddhism is the Avatamsaka Sutra or the Sutra of the Garland of Buddhas. Trying to summarize it in a few words is like trying to summarize a person by saying she's female. With this disclaimer as a protective shield, here goes. The sutra is basically a teaching about how everything is utterly connected to everything else. "Mutually unobstructed interpenetration" is the way the sutra puts it. The human mind (brace yourself for this next bit) is the universe itself and is identical to the Buddha. In other words, Buddha, mind, all sentient beings, are the same.

At some point, whatever your spiritual practice, sticking with it will open up a shift in understanding. The main thing is that the sutra is deeply liberating. It is hard to imagine a truth stronger than, "We're all Buddha."

Hwaomsa was built by an Avatamsaka Sutra fanatic. In the seventh century a monk named Ui-sang went to China to study under Zen masters. There he fell in love with the sutra. Hard. He would sing love songs to it, yearn to be chanting it day and night, sleep with it. Coming home to Korea he settled on the northern slope of Mt. Chiri, in a teeny temple that had been built in 554 A.D. Ui-sang expanded the temple in 634 A.D. and set about carving the entire sutra into stone. True to their pattern of pillaging, the Japanese invaded about a thousand years later, smashing the stone blocks to smithereens.

Once the invaders left, the surviving monks carefully collected all the stone pieces they could find and enshrined them in Hwaomsa's main hall. They also dedicated the temple to Vairocana, the Buddha who embodies the wisdom of universal law, the cosmic Buddha of the sutra.

The temple is majestic. Everything is oversized—the statues, the pagodas, the halls. The pagodas alone are three-story foundations held up by four massive lions. A good place to abandon aches, pains, fears, and major irritants.

In a compound dripping with spirituality and sacrifice for the greater good, one would expect the place to give other miracle hot spots such as Lourdes a run for their money. Hwaomsa does. Countless miracles are believed to have taken place there, from the healing of life-threatening diseases, to changing weather patterns, to sucking the insanity out of people's brains. I seemed to be slightly less smelly myself. And the headache that was following me around by that point in the pilgrimage went away. Since one never knows when the next big miracle will strike, the temple is understandably busy.

Hwaomsa was an oasis in a desert of crankiness. Refreshed from our visit we moved on.

* * *

Hiking again, Sunim turned back to us. "I'm trying to do three years of correcting in thirty days," he said. Oh really? No evil thoughts, no evil thoughts, no evil thoughts. But later, he told us stories to keep our minds occupied. Like while we waited for a ride or were offered tea Sunim would spontaneously start telling us stories about the difficulties the monks and nuns have faced in keeping Buddhism alive in Korea. Stories of the Korean war were particularly painful. The North Korean soldiers would go to the South Korean temples for food at night. When the South Korean police found out they gave the monks grenades to kill the North Koreans. The monks just threw them away. As the war went on North Korean soldiers showed up planning to kill the monks. In one temple the head monk demanded he be allowed to wear his robe so he could die in a dignified manner. When he put it on the soldiers didn't have the heart to kill him. The human capacity for courage is really something.

Chapter Nine

G.J. P'arang

Journal entry: September 12, 1999, Naesosa

"For some reason I keep thinking about the chapter on joy in the Dhammapada, about how we need to live in joy no matter what. It looks so easy on paper. Sure, I'll live in joy. Just don't throw any curve balls. Don't surprise me. Don't make me work hard. And for sure don't make me go for three weeks without pizza. Then I'm in. But only then. The hardest thing is to not count minutes. I miss Jamie and Sarth desperately. Hope they are okay, not that there is anything I can do if they aren't. God, I hope this is dharma. Sure is feeling more like a hell realm whenever I lose my grip on 'don't know' mind, which is just about every other minute."

While we were staying at Hwaomsa deep in the mountains, Haju and I popped up at the first sound of the *moktak*, as we did every morning. Folding our bedding, packing our backpacks, brushing our teeth, and walking quickly to the meditation hall, we immediately started doing prostrations, stopping at ninety-five as the monks began to enter the room.

Sunim came into the room and stood behind me.

As we started doing additional prostrations with the monks, a whack! Sunim had grabbed at my kasa—I think to try to straighten it because it wasn't on straight—and whacked me on the cheek instead. The sound reverberated throughout the hall. I was stunned. For a split second I didn't move. Then, thinking it was just a mistake on Sunim's part I started doing prostrations again. Whack! He did it again! I finished the morning service with the monks. Then, furious, walked across the courtyard to our rooms. Haju was nowhere to be seen. I put my kasa in Sunim's room and went to take a cool shower. Then I was ready to travel, vows be damned.

Coming back I saw Sunim on the porch.

"Please sit down Sunim," I invited him. He did. It was pitch black. Many of the monks had gone back to their rooms to get some sleep before breakfast. I was shaking with anger. He had, I told him, crossed my boundaries. He could not touch me again, ever. There had already been several instances of his shoving Haju during the journey. Each time I had been uneasy and felt an adrenaline rush. I wanted to intervene. Twice I almost did but Haju hadn't reacted at all. In an effort to honor her decision I would stand next to her trying not to cry. Sometimes I would get mad at Haju. Why didn't she defend herself? This wasn't dharma. This was an angry man looking for a human punching bag. There was a difference.

Sunim's response to my outburst was to point out that I was wearing my kasa wrong. I didn't bother to say that I had been wearing a kasa beside him for years or that the reason the kasas slipped was because we weren't wearing the right robes, the ones with the high collars that kept them in place.

I took the kasa off.

I said, "You could have whispered instructions instead of whacking me."

Him: "The monks straighten out the nuns' things here."

Me: "Not like that they don't."

Him: "I'm doing my best. Please wear the kasa. You haven't spent a lot of time with me and I am trying to make three years of corrections in thirty days."

Me: "No kasa. You are correcting so much that anything I can do to decrease the correction factor I'll do."

I was desperate to get rid of this thing that would cause him to yell at Haju or me. Of course, by this point in the trip, I was desperate to get rid of anything that would make him yell at us. I could only think, "Get rid of it. Put it somewhere else; anywhere except on my body. Someplace where it wouldn't trigger more anger or another whack. I folded it up and set it carefully in a corner of Sunim's room.

I was furious. Why would I wear something to honor a person who clearly wasn't respecting our effort? Seconds spread into timelessness. I could barely breathe. Neither of us moved.

Haju had come to kneel beside me. She didn't move either.

"There is no fire like passion, no crime like hatred." There it was again, the joy chapter from the Dhammapada. Over and over in my head. Finally we just stood up. Sunim went into his room. I walked through the temple grounds. They were completely quiet, lit by the stars. Here I was walking through sacred ground, my heart ripped open. I had trusted Sunim. Yes he yelled, yes he got angry. I never thought he would do anything to me physically. He was just straightening my kasa he said. It just didn't wash. Sunim had been angry, really angry, in that meditation hall. And it all came out at me. He knew it and I knew it and explaining it away didn't change what happened.

Pacing back and forth in front of the meditation hall I wanted to click my heels three times. I didn't even care where I landed. Anywhere was better than this. Where was the man's kindness and compassion? I sat on the steps of the hall, my head in my hands. Told myself to pay attention to the Dhammapada, to let things be, to just do my practice.

I walked back into our little room where Haju was sitting. Neither of us spoke. I lay down and waited for breakfast which wasn't for two hours. Feeling calmer I went into Sunim's room after he and Kaeo had left for the meal and took the kasa back. One painful incident was not going to destroy my love and respect for the tradition. I reminded myself that I had vowed to finish the trip partly so Haju could do the whole pilgrimage. Without another woman she would have to leave.

At breakfast, still raw, I couldn't even look at anyone, too afraid I would burst into tears. Sunim's behavior felt like such a betrayal. After breakfast we packed and started walking to the next temple, none of us talking. Only Kaeo came up to me and looked into my eyes. In his was deep compassion and concern. He had heard everything on the porch. We had an entire conversation just looking at each other, him telling me it was okay, and my saying I would be all right.

I remembered my sendoff present from my friend David. He rented *G.I. Jane* for me. In it Demi Moore shaves her head as a part of her Navy Seal training. I think that's the part David thought would help me. But a later scene helped more. In it Jane is fighting with her commander. He has beaten her to a bloody pulp as a part of the training, with clear instructions to the rest of her squad not to lift a finger to help her. They are in agony as they watch him go after her. Finally, it looks like she is dead. Suddenly she looks him in the eye and says those supremely eloquent words. "Suck my dick." And he knows he's done his job. She'll make it.

We all have our moments.

Too bad they're so painful.

As we made our way back down the mountain to board the bus to Songgwangsa all was quiet. No chatting. No smiles. We were about to climb onto the bus when a woman ran up to us, breathless. She chattered at Kaeo. He chattered back. She ran off. About two minutes later, as the bus was about to pull out, there she was again pounding on the door. The bus driver opened it and she shoved a bag at Kaeo and walked away. In it was a glass of fresh orange juice for each of us. It had been about ten days since the last taste of anything citrus. I tried to make mine last for the whole ride.

There it was again. Pure kindness popping out of nowhere. Life just wasn't black and white even when I wanted it to be.

As we rocked up the next series of mountains I had a million thoughts. Run away. Run away. Stay with it. Stay with it. Screw that. Run away while you can. I can't leave Haju. Sunim's just doing his best. No he isn't. He's a grinch. I just watched the fury until there was quiet. I hated what I was seeing about us. Forget Sunim. I hated what I was seeing about me. I had no idea I was such a whiner. Whine about this. Whine about that. And how deeply I resist something when I'm unsure where it is taking me. How I use anger for energy. And righteousness for anger. Sunim really was just being Sunim. If he hadn't whacked me then, it would have happened sooner or later. I needed to see just how angry I could get, and I needed to see how getting angry, that angry, can still be okay. It was honest and it was natural. What I did with it was the real test.

In the olden days, I knew, I would have left. I would have stomped off that mountain cursing Sunim with every step, VISA card in hand, hitching a ride to the nearest train station. Now I saw Sunim's own exhaustion and frustration and, I do believe, embarrassment, and how they stemmed from so many of the actions of these two Western women stumbling their way through Korea's mountains. It didn't make his behavior okay. May the man never again straighten a piece of clothing on my body in this life or any of the rest we'll probably spend together. But it made it comprehensible.

I remembered going to a marriage counselor years ago and a startling piece of advice: If things are really good sixty percent of the time, he said, you have an excellent marriage. So this must be an excellent trip. I found his percentage pretty hard to believe but then again I was raised on Cinderella.

Thoughts subsiding, suddenly "just this" was back. It was like my practice had its own life. Given any opening it would take over. All of the effort of the first few weeks was returning to protect me. "Just this" was the blanket around my shoulders and the buffer my body-mind needed. Once it kicked in I couldn't get the furious thoughts back when I tried.

Instead there was only this quiet sort of nonstruggling feeling like when you sit down in your favorite chair after a long hard day and just stare at what's in front of you until someone says, "Everything okay?" and you say, "Yeah," without any other explanation because it really is. That kind of quiet.

* * *

Songgwangsa made up for many of our trials and difficulties up to that point. Everything was so clean and bright. Everything was rainbow colors and all of the gazillions of Bodhisattvas and Buddhas (okay, a slight exaggeration) in the pictures had halos! (East meets West.) The clusters of buildings were like flower blossoms in a bouquet held by Quanseum Posal, an offering to humans yearning to find their own enlightened hearts.

When you look down at the temple compound from the mountains above, the roofs look like a bunch of dominoes that have been dropped onto a tan and green rug. They are squished close together, smaller relative to the other temples we visited, and aimed in all sorts of directions. Like a Matisse painting dropped in the middle of Mother Nature. Beautiful. No, more than beautiful. Breathtaking. Robert Buswell, an American who studied at the temple some years back, seems to have had a similar reaction: "From the small village below the temple, pilgrims to Songgwangsa start a gentle, half mile climb to the monastery. The trail winds through pure forest, following the stream that runs alongside the monastery. Just below the main temple complex there is a field of stone stelae, each about 8 feet in height, on which are inscribed records of the monastery's history." (Robert Buswell, *The Zen Monastic Experience*, Princeton University Press, Princeton, 1992, p. 49) In the main Buddha hall is a twenty-five-foot wooden altar, with Vairocana staring down at you. Vairocana is kept company by a huge scroll painting of the Buddhist pantheon that sort of looks like a class reunion picture where you are trying to fit anyone you've ever known in any lifetime into one picture. Stupas party in a field nearby. I stopped counting after I reached thirty.

Maybe because we were on the second half of the pilgrimage or maybe it was because the monks were so generous and I had perfected sleeping anywhere on any ground, Songgwangsa was the temple I didn't want to leave. Ever. (Not to brag, I was also able to catch flies in my hand by then, a useful skill for eating in public places. These pilgrimages offer so much.)

Songgwangsa was originally built by one of Korea's great Zen masters, Chinul. Chinul is special because he managed to attain enlightenment without the help of a teacher. Studying sutras did the trick. As the story goes, one day during a rest period he was reading the Platform Sutra of the 6th Patriarch and achieved spontaneous enlightenment upon reading the passage, "(our) self-nature of suchness is always free and untainted." He's about the only person who has openly managed such a feat. Chinul cared deeply about Buddhism and how it could help people find a center of genuine peace. Surrounded by political infighting among the various Buddhist sects that had sprung up in Korea by the twelfth century, he was determined that the sects should all be woven together into one happy Buddhist family. It's a wonder he wasn't killed. Starting in 1190, it took thirty years of effort to make any headway into his vision, finally culminating in a single place where all the monks were invited to come to practice. That place is Songgwangsa.

People started showing up at the door as fast as word got out. The parade hasn't stopped. Korea's most revered master of the twentieth century, Master Kusan (1901–1983), set up Korea's first international Zen Center on Chinul's temple grounds so foreigners would have a place to study the Korean Way of Zen. Some of the West's first round of significant Buddhist teachers, including Robert Buswell and Martine and Stephen Batchelor, studied there. He'll be in good hands.

Our room was wonderful: woodenlattice work covered with rice paper let a hazy light into the room—almost like a night-light only it was a whole wall. Rice paper for wallpaper. A thick yellow plastic floor with a barely discernible pattern of herons and suns.

Rules were still thrown at us. "Don't stand in the middle of the meditation hall. It's for senior monks." Conveyed while I stood at the door of the meditation hall trying to recall if there had been a single hall where I *hadn't* stood in its middle. Oh well. Just this.

It was at Songgwangsa that I learned that typically it is only the beginner-beginner monks who do 108 prostrations each day. Usually the monks don't do any prostrations. This, after twelve years of doing them. Hmm. And kasas? Also only worn by the junior monks. Sunim really was introducing a new monastic model to them and to us. We were two middle-aged women doing more prostrations than anyone else as a demonstration of determination and sincerity. No one could argue with our efforts. The kasas were a first foothold in a monastic tradition that has been male-only for over a thousand years in Korea. And there we were wearing them every day. No wonder Sunim was so sensitive, so quick to react to our every mistake. I started to see the pilgrimage from a whole different perspective. It wasn't just about Haju and me doing our best, it was about introducing women as monks, rather than nuns. I needed to be more skillful for the women who would follow our footsteps.

People who have done pilgrimages tell me that despair always hits at some point. One becomes overwhelmed with a combination of exhaustion and shattered expectations when things get tough and stay tough. Ironically, it hit me when we were at beautiful sweet Songgwangsa. A teacher I trusted failed me, failed us. What I thought the pilgrimage was going to be like was so far off the mark it was on another planet. I had failed Haju by being angry, frustrated, and noisy. We had both failed to be gracious, graceful monastics.

I was miserable.

Determined not to drown in the waves of sheer anguish, I tried to conjure up stories I had heard about other people who had made it through such darkness. "Millions of pilgrims have been right here," I told myself. Sitting outside of a bookstore waiting for Sunim I searched my brain for a story to help me. Nothing. I gave up. Let "just this" take over. It was feeble but it was there.

If I had stayed with my search I would have remembered the story of Don Miguel Ruiz. He's a doctor who almost killed himself one night driving head-on into a concrete wall. Somehow surviving, he decided to live his life in a totally different way, making four vows to himself: to be impeccable with his word; to stop taking anything personally; to stop making assumptions; and to always do his best. He called them the Four Agreements. I loved his sheer determination to get through any dark nights of the soul using the agreements: "That's why you need to be a great hunter, a great warrior, who can defend these Four Agreements with your life. Your happiness, your freedom, your entire way of living depends on it. The warrior's goal is to transcend this world... I didn't expect that I could do it at first. I have fallen many times, but I stood up and kept going. And I fell again and I kept going. I didn't feel sorry for myself. There was no way that I felt sorry for myself. I said, 'If I fall, I am strong enough, I'm intelligent enough, I can do it.' I stood up and kept going. I fell and I kept going and going, and each time it became easier and easier." (Don Miguel Ruiz, *The Four Agreements*, Amber-Allen Publishing, San Rafael, California, 1994, pp. 89-90)

We also got sick right about then. First Haju's stomach. Then Kaeo's headache was so bad, he was nauseated and dizzy, barely coping with his pain. Me? I got a good, juicy I'll-never-leave-you-no-matter-what-you-do urinary tract infection. (Later I learned that I had actually been contending with a combination of pneumonia and chronic fatigue—the urinary infection was just one aspect of the infection that had decided to

call my body home. Makes me feel better about all the whining somehow.) I started dreaming about cranberry juice.

Being sick didn't matter. We never slowed our pace.

After Songgwangsa we came to Naesosa, a small temple in a bowl-
shaped valley surrounded by mountains and pastures, the smell of the
ocean nearby. Since we were closing in on the last part of the pilgrimage it didn't matter that we were barely greeted, offered a room as an
afterthought, and felt truly unwelcome at meals. By then our focus had
shifted to figuring out how to wash our totally filthy clothes. The water
in the little washtub turned an ominous, thick gray-greenish color when
I put my one pair of gray pants into it. I stared at the patterns in the water
as long as I could, confident a genie would appear, until finally the
smell of food told me I'd better finish. I rinsed out the pants and put
them on soaking wet. I remember thinking that Naesosa would probably not have seemed beautiful to me if I had been wearing clean clothes.
But I wasn't so it wasn't.

From there we moved into higher mountains, the ones that hold up
the sky. I figured the worst had to be over. Except that it started to rain
harder and harder on our way up. The tiny hermitage we were headed
for was a vertical climb, along the washed-out trail, amid falling rocks.
It was actually quite dangerous. Sunim decided that we would simply
hitch a ride up the mountain in the hermitage's supply conveyor. This
was a four-foot rectangular open-topped metal box hooked to a cable
and a simple pulley system. The cable pulled the box up the spine of the
mountain.

First Kaeo got in. He squished himself as far to the front as he could,
knees to chin. Then Sunim. Same squishing. Then Haju. Then me, with
all our backpacks. When the motor cable started, Sunim looked at me.
"Don't let our things fall out, P'arang."

We started moving up the mountain. The rain made everything slippery and there was only the edge of the box to grasp. After about three

minutes I looked behind us. You couldn't see the mountain behind the box, it was that steep. Looking ahead of us, we could only see the tops of some trees beside us. To our right there wasn't anything to see. To our left, more treetops.

It was too terrifying to even think. I just did my practice, knowing that a single slip of the cable and we would all die.

Halfway up, the cable started to shudder. There was too much weight in the box. We slowed to a stop. It felt like we were starting to slip. If we did I knew we would flip off the cliff. It was all I could do to hold onto the box and some of our things. The backpacks and camera were sliding backwards.

Silence everywhere. Not even the sound of breathing. Calmly I whispered goodbye to my daughter. Told her I love her. Ditto to my son, family, friends. I felt a strange, overwhelming sense of deep gratitude for everything my life had been. It made me warm. Then I just hunkered down to *hwadu* (to "what is it?") putting all of my concentration into the question, refusing to let go of any part of it. What was amazing was the total absence of fear. I couldn't find it anywhere.

A small shudder and the box began to move again, inching its way up the mountain. At the top, Sunim casually mentioned that we would walk down the mountain the next day instead of using the box.

Being face to face with dying was no big deal. It was past tense as soon as we hit solid ground. I had always wondered what it would be like to really stare death in the face. What would I think? Or do? Would I be calm or hysterical? Would I pee all over myself and then faint away? It turned out that facing death was just like facing life. As long as I was clear about what was happening I could just be with it. In that space fear didn't have a chance. Without fear crowding my brain, my overwhelming feeling was gratitude.

The hermitage at the top of the mountain was tiny. It was basically three small buildings. The first, about twenty giant steps away from a cliff

overlooking an enormous mountain range, was about the size of a dou-
ble-wide mobile home. In it was housed a community dining room,
kitchen, and head monk's quarters. About a hundred feet above it, at the
top of the mountain path, was a set of tiny square rooms, maybe a dozen,
inside a slightly longer building. Beside that was a meditation hall which
we never saw because some young monks had spontaneously decided to
continue a three-month intensive retreat indefinitely. Beside the commu-
nal kitchen, and down a steep animal path, was a brand new outhouse,
complete with a proper toilet seat!

By the time we got there we were tired. Facing death does that, I
guess. We ate a little, and went to our respective rooms with strict instructions to be silent so as not to disturb the monks. Except for stumbling up
and down the path to the outhouse in the dark, we did okay.

In the morning we woke up before dawn and watched posalnims for-
aging for greens for breakfast. The breakfast table was set with a half-
dozen bowls filled with different vegetables that looked suspiciously like
weeds, and wild mushrooms that looked suspiciously like psilocybin.
Hey, we didn't care. We were alive. We ate every bite. Delicious.

Just as we were leaving the hermitage the young abbot insisted that
we stop to have tea with him. Four cups each of green tea. (Like shots of
whiskey, only for energy!)

Walking "down" the mountain turned into a four-and-a-half-hour
hike up and down several peaks to get to a place where we could catch
a bus to the next temple on Sunim's mental itinerary. For the first hour we
were looking down on clouds so close you felt you could jump on them
and ride across the valleys. We had a few encounters that would have
been terrifying had we not played death by cable car the previous day.
The steep rock walls forced us to climb straight up. We used our hands
and feet to push ourselves forward even as the weight of our backpacks
pulled us backward. Tiny yellow and bright blue flowers greeted our
every turn and stories from Sunim kept us going.

By the time of our second rest stop we were out of food and water. It was really hot and mountain peaks seemed to go on forever. When my legs started to turn to jelly, I remembered my friend Sanho telling me that "You climb mountains with your stomach." So I did. It helped.

In the middle of it all Sunim stopped suddenly and looked at me. "P'arang, you could learn something from Haju. She does difficult things easy." And it was true. There she was grinning from ear to ear having the time of her life, climbing those rocks like a veritable mountain goat. Have I mentioned that she is closing in on sixty? It got me to thinking about enlightenment and our almost mountain slide. I remembered another teaching by Dainin Katagiri that really struck home:

"For instance, let us imagine that you are climbing up a mountain cliff. That situation is just like being on the verge of life and death. There is no way to escape; you cannot complain. If you are there all you have to do is just be there. If you act instinctively, you could die. If you are nervous you could die. Should you depend on your intellect you could also die. So you have to depend on the mountain, your mind, and the circumstances. You have to watch carefully and understand. Your consciousness must be clear and know what is going on there. Then, after using your best understanding, your body and mind should depend on just one step. This is action. This is the process of one step without being nervous about what will happen in the next moment, or thinking about when you will reach the peak, or how far down the bottom is, or who is climbing or how much farther you can keep going like this, or that you could die. There is nothing to think about, nothing to depend on. All we have to do is just be there using all the things we already have: consciousness, mind, mountain, and weather. Then we have to act. Just take one step, a pretty simple step." (Dainin Katagiri, *Return to Silence: Zen Practice in Daily Life,* Shambala, Boston and London, 1988, p. 106)

I thought about how we Westerners make enlightenment a goal so we have some way of wrapping our arms around it. We want it to be an obvious accomplishment that will somehow define us as special, although, of course, we're trying not to be. Even when rushes of energy flew up my spine in surprise moments, I knew it wasn't enlightenment. It wasn't the awakeness that Buddha taught. I was still oh so me, still getting a kick out of the rush, still wanting more. And enlightenment isn't all the extrasensory stuff that we want to call enlightenment, those psychic moments, that sense that maybe we really can create miracles. Stone mountains roaring and fish flying aren't worth squat as long as some part of "me" is watching, looking for karmic points. It's enough to make a head hurt.

Finally, we made it to the bottom of the last trail, where there was a tiny store. I remember thinking that maybe fish do fly, I was so surprised to see it. Without a word Sunim went in, and a couple of long minutes later walked out with an armful of bottles of water. We couldn't drink them fast enough. He also had a Coca Cola. Handed it to me. Life was good again.

Rehydrated, we found a bus stop and a bus. Then, sitting on the bus, filthy (as in you couldn't scrape the dirt on my face and neck off even if you had one-inch nails shaped like sabers), I had a sudden sinking feeling. It was physical—not dizzy, sinking; well, maybe a little dizziness, except my body didn't move. Instead I felt enveloped in a huge quiet place. Actually it was more like there was a huge quiet place without a "me" observing and judging and categorizing every single little thing. The huge quiet space was just sitting. In that moment all the kicking and screaming and bitching that had been running me disappeared. I was in the land of "now" where, I gotta tell you, it's all poetry.

Colors were brighter and sounds were louder and sharper. I heard so many birds that, for a moment, I thought someone was playing a tape of bird songs on the bus. Then the most fascinating thing in the whole world was the conversation between the young bus driver and an old old woman with a cane sitting in the front seat across from him. It was like watching an opera. When Sunim came out of the little store—a South Korean version of a 7-Eleven—for the second time with more bottles of water, his quick steps were just like a tap dance right out of a Broadway musical. The whole world was happy. I half expected to see cartoon characters pop out from behind trees singing, "It's a small world after all," and an airplane with a banner saying that Disneyworld Korea hoped we had enjoyed our visit.

Everything was okay. How wonderful it was to be free of all the ego junk, even if it was just for a moment in time. As weird as this sounds, my heart felt like it would burst. I couldn't wait to get home to see what it was like to just clean, just cook, just work.

Maybe those mushrooms *were* hallucinogenic.

Chapter Ten

Clarity and Compassion, Care of Korea

Journal entry: September 19, 1999, on the express train to Seoul

"We just got on the express train to Seoul. Since it is the hundredth anniversary of the train system we got a free quarter cup of coffee to swallow down. Also a miniature manicure set. With one swig of the coffee all is forgiven. We ARE what we think and it's better not to think on less than four hours of sleep a night! Sunim is what he is. This moment is it... Many of the temples have large panels depicting the oxherding pictures on them. Teaching pictures about the phases of 'enlightenment' a human can experience. The panels are eight feet long and maybe two feet high. Bright colors. An adorable kid playing the role of the human. At the end of his journey through the pictures he is compassion.

"What a metaphor for this pilgrimage. In the beginning only flashes of compassion. Mostly head tripping—whining, judging. Then there's the miserable part, the just keep rowing part, the don't quit part where through a cloud of exhaustion and general pissed offness you just have to wonder what happened to the compassion part. Maybe it was never there in the first place. Mind fights for survival, for control. Everything that could possibly be wrong with your teacher and the situation is. If he is a grinch this is an easy exercise.

"You can go nuts with all the planning, being homesick, and judging and if your ego is really fighting for its life you'll probably get sick as well. Urinary tract infections are effective here.

125

"But the heart-driven moments keep you going. A posalnim gives you her only set of prayer beads. Another gets up in the middle of the night to make egg salad sandwiches for breakfast, knowing how desperate you are to eat something other than rice. You see an old woman your grand-mother's age dragging fifty pounds of grain onto a bus—inch by inch— only to stand at the front joking with the young studly driver who clearly enjoys her company. And you keep doing your practice because frankly there isn't anything else to do. And suddenly your compassionate heart has a shot at winning the race of what will control your life. The longer the trip, the more your heart has a chance to impact your moments until finally, in a moment of utter exhaustion, you realize that you've disap-peared into a heart of compassion. And not only that, there's a wisdom in that place that will never let you down. Not ever. It's time to go home."

Lines from the Diamond Sutra are crammed around the edges of my Korean journal. Suon Sunim taught me about that, about just writing down the lines of a sutra as a form of meditation practice. He fills a large blank page every morning, top to bottom. I figured I'd try it. First, all the lines were horizontal and written from left to right the way we were taught in grade school. Then I started writing around in circles and then in squares. If there had been more room I would have drawn pictures with the words. After a couple of days I just pulled out my pen whenever we were near a source of blank paper—the backs of receipts, wrapping paper, food wrappings. I just grabbed a pen or pencil and started copy-ing lines. It started to make sense after about the fiftieth rendition.

The Diamond Sutra, or Sutra of the Diamond Cutter of Supreme Wis-dom, is a big deal. In many monasteries it is chanted in its entirety every morning. We read it every day in the second year of the Maitreya Bud-dhist Seminary. The instruction was to read it out loud as fast as we could, trying to feel it rather than understand it. Sometimes I felt like I

126

understood it but mostly I would just do it to get it over with, another ritual that I would never understand.

Basically, the sutra teaches that all phenomenal appearances aren't ultimate reality, they are illusions and every practitioner of meditation needs to regard everything as illusion, as "empty, devoid of self, and tranquil." See what I mean about not obvious? If everything is simply illusion then why should we do anything but sit in a barcalounger with a six-pack watching reruns of *Whose Line Is It Anyway?* I chose to ignore such an obvious question while I was in the seminary, deciding that something must have been left out in the translation. I figured our seminary version was probably just a Cliff Notes version of the teaching, the one where the translator forgot to give us the punchline.

But the bloody thing kept reappearing during the last year of the seminary and in the seven years since. Different teachers, ones I respected, kept calling the Diamond Sutra a seminal teaching. It seemed as though every time I opened a book about Buddhism, the "diamond" aspect of the sutra was always emphasized. Like a diamond, the sutra fearlessly "slices away all unnecessary conceptualization and brings one to the further shore of enlightenment." (*The Shambala Dictionary of Buddhism and Zen*, Shambala, Boston, 1991, p. 57)

I guess.

In Korea I took another run at it by keeping it with me all the time and reading it over and over whenever we were sitting somewhere waiting for Sunim. Basically, the sutra is this sweet story about how Buddha, tired from a long day of teaching and begging for food, sits down to relax when one of his students, Subhuti, asks him a series of questions. First he wants to know what people like us, who sincerely want to "give rise to the highest, most fulfilled awakened mind" should use for our learning.

Then he asks for skills—what should we do to mature our thinking?

With 1,250 of his followers leaning in to hear his response, Buddha answers Subhuti and as he answers, the answer itself shifts. First, he says, if we want to be awake we have to lead all beings to their awakeness as well.

So far, so good.

And we have to be really generous.

Okay.

But then he goes for the jugular. If we do these things thinking that one person is helping another we're thrown out of the game. If we are generous to get points in the form of merit, recognition, good press, a better job—whatever—we're also screwed. If we are obvious about any of our behavior, looking for the slightest touch of fame (mea culpa), fortune, recognition, or even a thank-you, out of the game we go.

Instead, without any forethought, there should be instant compassion, instant acts of kindness, without any thought of reward. An example of such unplanned, thoughtless action goes something like this: Let's just say the left sleeve of the shirt you are wearing suddenly starts to burn. You will immediately swat out the fire with your other hand and cover the burnt arm with cold water or ointment or kisses or some combination of them all. Not for even a millisecond do you think, "Oh, I'm helping the left arm." You just automatically help. You just do it. Just this.

On returning from Korea I facilitated a seminar on forgiveness from a Buddhist perspective. The point of the seminar was to propose an alternative approach to "turning the other cheek." Since that has never worked for me, I figured I might have some company looking for other ways of dealing with a broken heart. Settling into the community room at the Crazy Wisdom bookstore and tearoom we worked through several basic Buddhist teachings: that all beings are precious, including us; that it helps to consider our interconnectedness when we think about painful situations; how knowing people's personal stories can help us at least understand their "unforgivable" behavior; that we need to "pull the arrow right out" instead of overanalyzing and criticizing and playing martyr, even when we have legitimate reasons to do all three.

About three quarters of the way through the class people started talking about some of the experiences that had driven them to the seminar. And how they were still having a really hard time forgiving. Their stories were pretty horrible. A small woman sitting against one wall talked about how she is being stalked. As an expert on this topic, having been stalked twice, I told her how I got rid of my two stalkers in what I thought were pretty harmless ways. The first one was easy. I just asked one of my men friends to record the "We're not in" message on my answering machine so mine wasn't the voice callers heard. That day was the last day I heard from stalker #1.

Stalker #2 was tougher. His favorite thing was to wait until after dark and then walk around my block all night, occasionally trying my windows to see if they were locked. Since he was doing this before my state had any stalking laws, the local police, while sympathetic, couldn't do much more than try to catch him in the act of breaking and entering.

That wouldn't do.

I asked a friend of mine, a hunter, if he would mind sitting on my couch with his shotgun, not to shoot the guy but to scare him away. We opened the blinds just enough for the stalker to see inside. My friend sat there all night, gun in his lap. We never saw the stalker again.

The woman looked at me and said, "I don't know anyone who would do that." In less than a millisecond two of the men in the room, complete strangers to her (I knew them) offered to stay at her house for as long as it took. A natural and spontaneous reaction on both their parts. No ego, only compassion. That's the essence of the Diamond Sutra.

But Buddha doesn't stop there. If Subhuti was going to ask the hard questions, he was going to give him hard answers:

"Thousands of lifetimes ago when my body was cut into pieces by King Kalinga I was not caught up in the idea of a self, a person, a living being, or a life span. If, at that time, I had been caught up in any of those ideas I would have felt anger and ill-will against the king... Subhuti, when a Bodhisattva gives rise to the unequalled mind of awakening, he has to give up all ideas. He cannot rely on forms when he gives rise to that mind, nor on sounds, smells, tastes, tactile objects, or objects of mind. He can only give rise to that mind that is not caught up in anything." (Thich Nhat Hanh, *The Diamond That Cuts Through Illusion: Commentaries on the Prajnaparamita Diamond Sutra*, Parallax Press, Berkeley, California, 1992, p. 13)

I probably chanted or reread the sutra fifty times by the end of our trip, partly out of desperation for something to read in English and partly because it somehow made more sense with each reading, not that I could ever say what it was, exactly, that was making more sense. Here's the thing. As long as my go-for-broke mind was kicked in I wanted explanations, about everything, about the sutra, about the trip, about the behaviors, about the rituals. I wanted respectful discourses taking place at the end of a lovely, dry, stroll-filled day. Not exhaustion.

But the trip was literally squeezing everything right out of me. Surviving meant letting go of everything. No expectations. Just paying attention as best I could and letting whatever happened happen.

As I was thinking about forms and formlessness à la the Diamond Sutra one morning, Sunim suddenly started talking about both (he was reading my mind again). He said we eventually grow out of the forms, out of dualism. Even so, forms have their uses. They provide an environment where people can express their emotions. For example, if every morning chanting is done a particular way and suddenly the resident "mad monk" starts singing techno pop it has quite an impact. But if any song could be sung at any time how could he demonstrate his awakeness? Even the way we opened the sliding doors to our bedrooms was a metaphor for our own awakening. Were we careful and quiet? Graceful? Opening them with a sudden shout? As our understanding deepened, he promised that we would better know how to deal with each situation we found ourselves in. We would know when to follow every single rule of the monastery and when it didn't matter. As a result, every experience would be a brand new experience. We would understand that embracing life is about paying the closest possible attention to all of it, changing the rules when they need to be changed, and keeping them when they need to be kept. "It's common sense," he said.

That's awakeness.

* * *

Right before we headed back to Seoul, Sunim took us to the teeniest hermitage of all, built on the edge of yet another cliff. It was home to a single nun and a young businessman who was spending a hundred days with her doing chanting or *kido* practice. The nun was known for her kido chanting. To get there we had to take a long bus ride, then a long car ride, then we had to climb hundreds and hundreds of steps straight up the mountainside in the dark. When we finally made it to the top, we looked down over a port filled with lights from tanker ships. They looked like small toy boats in a McDonald's children's meal.

On the way there Sunim told us stories of the power of kido practice to heal people. One was about a woman who was deathly ill. Neither doctors nor medications had been able to help her. Finally in desperation her husband suggested kido. After chanting for a hundred days not only was she healed, but she had developed her own healing powers and is still healing people today. Her husband wanted her to charge money for her work but she refused. Whenever money was involved, her brain fogged up, she said.

To raise *bodhicitta* (awakening mind) some monks and nuns do kido all the time. Even lay people do 100, 1000, or even 100,000 days of chanting as a form of purification practice. Sunim says it saves people's sanity and I believe he's right. He wanted us to experience its power first hand to get a taste of transcendence, he said. In that space we would see that everything passes, out of its emptiness would grow a deeper compassion, out of the compassion, wisdom, and so we might get a taste of the Diamond Sutra.

So we climbed the last mountain. An upset stomach meant I was living on rice, sprouts, tea, and a little fruit. The air was fine and the energy high. The young nun met us at the top. She was doing kido all day, in two-hour intervals. Haju and I joined in, starting with a two-hour session from 3 A.M. to 5 A.M. At first it felt rather awkward. The tiny room was dark, dimly lit by candles. We couldn't quite see if the nun was standing, kneeling, or doing prostrations, but we started anyway. At first we were a bit wobbly, then with a sort of breathiness, our voices merged and we were the whole world chanting and swaying through the night. Negative emotions dropped away. So did our tiredness. We were surrounded by a sensation of compassion all around us that was deeply comforting.

Once again we were so high in the mountains that I had dreams about them. In the dreams each peak was an enormous earth mother cradling everyone on it so no one would fall into space. When I asked one of the peaks why they were willing to take care of us for millions of years when all we did was stab them and poison them and pee on them and ignore them she said, "You are all Buddha," and put an extra blanket on me because, for once, I was cold.

The next night there was so much energy running through my body I couldn't sleep. It felt like someone had stuck my hand into some invisible electrical current. I kept trying not to laugh. Sitting outside on a ledge, stars at eye level, rushes of energy kept moving up my spine trying to blast out of the top of my head. Not yet, not yet, I kept saying. It was like trying not to have a full-body orgasm—sooner or later you know you'll have to give in.

A different passage from the Dhammapada started popping up inside the waves of energy:

Wakefulness is the way to life.

The fool sleeps

As if he were already dead,

But the master is awake

And he lives forever.

He watches.

He is clear.

How happy he is!

For he sees that wakefulness is life.

How happy he is,

Following the path of the awakened.

(*The Dhammapada, The Sayings of the Buddha*, A New Rendering by Thomas Byrom, Vintage Books, New York, 1976, pp. 9-10)

Aha! Mindfulness is what leads to letting go—to the dropping away of everything we think we are. That's why Sunim kept yelling at us to pay attention to everything every time we turned around. Mindfulness is the path into the Diamond Sutra! Every minute the monks and nuns were teaching us the path. We just had to be smart enough to pay attention.

Wowie!

Colors, colors, colors were all around us. As the energy grew, colors got more vivid, like some Disney artist went wild around the mountains. Pink, really pink flowers and soft lime green ferns grew out of gray rocks surrounding a small fountain. The water in the fountain reflected the brilliant foliage and caught the clouds passing overhead. Pale pink lotus flowers grew out of a deep green-brown trough in the middle of a dirt courtyard like a still life that had been painted just for us.

Monks and nuns were vividly different. Some who worked the land were dark skinned with rough, earth-colored callused hands. The pale ones who ran the monasteries spent their days mostly indoors in cleaner, brighter robes. Artist monks had splashes of colored pigments under their nails and on their clothes. (I loved that.) Musician monks, temple cooks, professor nuns: all shapes and sizes and subtle shades. For each, a unique path into their own enlightenment. Even though they shared basic training in the form of meditation, prostrations, chanting, and sutra study, they all had different means for finding the way. What mattered was the paying attention, the watchfulness, the "just this"ness of their minds, the diamond cutting through delusion.

How freeing! I realized that, in that place of compassion-filled mindfulness, artists could find their own enlightened hearts through art, musicians through music, poets through poetry, farmers through farming. An old dharma brother of Sunim's, who loved chanting "Om Mani Padme Hum," chanted his way into awakeness. Other monks and nuns used koans, but not like they do in Japan. Instead of moving from one question to the next, they stuck with "What is it?" for a lifetime. It is said that once you have the answer to that question you'll understand the answer to 700 more *hwadus* without any effort.

Learning the mechanics of meditation practice, the rituals and traditions, was only a first step, the raft across the river. After that each of us has to find our own practice, the one that works for us.

I chose writing.

If there isn't an obvious path, you can always be a temple cook. Enlightenment is guaranteed if you stay nine years. One monk told us that kido practice would help us no matter what path we ended up choosing. In fact, if we wanted to accomplish something in particular we just needed to do chanting practice for three months and ten days. By the end of the chanting period, he told us, we would have become the manifestation of peace. People would respond to that. Our lives would work out. A temple would get built if we wanted to build a temple, family concerns would clear up if that was what was troubling us.

The monks and nuns we met were living proof of the power of the combination of formal training and mindfulness practice. So many had moved beyond such terrible tragedies that after a while, I stopped being surprised at the stories I heard. Some were orphans of war or famine. Some had a parent or sibling who had committed suicide. One elderly man had lost both his wife and his daughter. The daughter, a nun, had burned herself to death. His practice had saved his sanity. His generosity saved his life. The man glows.

Sitting on a rock ledge at the hermitage, reading the Diamond Sutra, the sentences seemed to dance on the pages. By that point "just this" was with me constantly. It felt like I had dharma back-up singers! There I was, mouthing the words of the sutra, "just this"ing along, and WHAM! Suddenly there was all this crazy happy energy. Everything is Buddha! Everyone is Buddha! After a flash of "Did someone slip me something at breakfast?" I had a sudden realization that the energy I had been hoping against hope would kick in had finally shown up on my exhausted doorstep. And everything changed, even though it was all the same. (This is starting to sound a little like St. Theresa on XTC, I know.) Every-thing *sparkled*. Colors brightened. Greens turned to emerald and reds were deeper, brighter, richer.

Buddhas kept appearing in so many fascinating forms. One was a woman tea master in Seoul who told us that more and more people are using the tea ceremony as a way to step back from worldly life. Drinking tea, she told us, provides a serene environment that is comforting.

* * *

How to make citrus tea: Cut up big chunks of oranges, lemons, and grapefruit. Put them in a big pot. Include the rinds. Cover them with water. Cook for hours over low heat. Sweeten with honey. Pour some of it into a teapot when you are ready for some comfort.

* * *

In a temple in Yosu, a city on the southern coast, a small elderly woman with a bent back, watering eyes, pure white hair, and gnarled hands demanded that I accept the only beads she owned—a brown plastic beaded rosary. When I tried to close my hands in a gesture of appreciation but no thank you, she stomped her foot and peeled open my hand, putting the beads there and closing my fingers over them.

In the same temple, there was a young woman living with her disabled son who befriended us. She and I kept each other company, sneaking into the washroom together to wash our clothes when everyone else was sleeping. I drew sketches on her journal pages; she wrote on mine. She didn't speak a word of English and I didn't think "hurry up" had a place in any of our mimed conversations, although I did manage to work in "thank you" a couple of times.

She gave me her wrist beads. I gave her mine. I wished I had more to give her but by then we were pretty much down to the clothes we were wearing. Looking back, I could have given her my copy of the Diamond Sutra even if she couldn't read it. It would have been a connection.

As we were leaving the temple compound she ran after our car, insisting that the driver stop. When he finally did and rolled down the back window where I was sitting, she thrust her hand in at me. In it was a four-leaf clover that had been pressed flat. If I could tape it on my heart I would.

Journal entry: September 20, 1999, Seoul

"What happens is that your life sorts itself out in the in-between moments...when I start to feel like I just have to move my legs for example. Or when we've been running to catch up with Sunim and he suddenly just stops. Right then everything just drops away but practice because on three to five hours of sleep a night, and with this kind of effort, there is only enough energy to do two things and one of those is staying alive. So the second may as well be spiritual practice unless you just want to keep revisiting your karmic habits like a broken record."

Filled with dharma energy and about as clearheaded as I'll ever be, in Yosu I found my mind replaying much of the trip, remembering things I hadn't realized were significant. For instance, the temples all had beautiful poems carved into the huge wooden boards that were nailed to their fronts. Some of the poems had five lines, some had seven. One of my favorites was about how sitting in the winter cold and wind makes one appreciate spring's cherry blossom. Amen to that. On another beam was this poem:

One house in the whole universe,

Single moment from time immemorial to the present now.

One master living in this house.

His face does not change throughout.

There it was again, my old friend the Diamond Sutra! It was like it was following me around, appearing at unexpected moments, in unexpected places.

And finally, in the last week of our journey, a kinder, gentler Sunim made himself evident. He was less angry, less critical. Sometimes he was even my best friend again, just like in the old pre-Korea days. We decided to try our hand at hitchhiking when it became clear, at one point, that we were definitely in the middle of nowhere. Sunim and I stood together, thumbs out, on the side of the road, while Haju waited for us in the shade. Instead, we attracted two adorable puppies who covered us with puppy kisses when we opened our arms to say good morning.

Later, as we were climbing another mountain, Sunim turned to me when we paused to catch our breath. "Your cousin is here to see you but she's shy. You have to let go of your human sensibilities so she'll feel secure enough to come out for a visit."

I actually knew what he meant: that our human sensibilities are only makeshift shells wrapped around pure Buddha nature. But mostly I was touched that he was still doing his best to point to the moon, even after I had howled at him like the wildest wolf cousin I've got. (There is an expression, "pointing to the moon," that means teachers can only direct us, we have to do our own work.)

Toward the trip's end we received word that we were going to be allowed to visit the nuns' college of Unmunsa. Stronger, feistier women don't exist anywhere. On the one hand they are taught to cultivate a strong sense of responsibility to the world, and on the other—transcendence. The young women spend every waking moment memorizing sutras, learning to cook, to farm, to arrange flowers. They are expected to master calligraphy and excel in their university studies. Semesters are year round with one or two three-day vacations which the young women mostly use to climb nearby mountains, meditate, and write letters. Every day they do repentance practice on behalf of people who have gone wrong. Occasionally a young nun will "fall into psychic tendencies" and become a healer. They were an interesting group. I wish they were running Congress.

Their compound was exquisitely beautiful in an if-Martha Stewart-was-a-Zen-master way. The first thing I noticed when I walked onto the campus was how spotlessly clean everything was. Nothing was out of place. Not a scrap of trash was visible. Not even gum wrappers, even though tourists find their way to the compound on a regular basis. No straggly plants, no brown leaves. Again there was dazzling color everywhere as though a liquid rainbow had spilled on the roofs and poured itself over everything: flowers, urns, rugs, and statues. All this against a background of golden brown dirt.

Walking across the campus we could see rooms full of young nuns, women in their teens and early twenties, studying. Their shaved heads were lowered in concentration as they memorized sutras in addition to the full course load of other subjects.

We were greeted by a spunky twenty-something who ushered us into a formal sitting parlor edged by floor-to-ceiling doors and long verandas on two sides. Orchids and antiques kept company with huge books of Buddhist literature, statues, and exquisitely brocade-covered couches and chairs, mostly pale yellow and creamy whites. There we met with one of the senior nuns, an older woman who is in charge of Unmunsa's curriculum. As she greeted us, she looked into Haju's eyes and then mine. She smiled a slight smile.

We sat together and drank tea. It was delicate, almost sweet, unlike anything I've ever tasted. Jasmine maybe. A young novice nun brought us plates of tea cookies, each surrounded with tiny flower blossoms. The attention to the tiniest detail was astonishing, down to the positioning of the flower blossoms on the plate. We drank slowly, Sunim and the older nun chatting a bit, and then we were escorted to our rooms where we could rest (rest!) until lunch.

Outside all of the young nuns were hard at work. Manual work is interspersed between classes to help the students sustain their concentration and keep their energy high. To a person they were giving their chores their complete attention. Some were scrubbing floors on their hands and knees, some were watering plants, some polishing altar pieces. Classical music was piped over a loudspeaker system.

The young attendant nun walked us to a lovely building in a far corner of the campus. It had just been built and even smelled new. It had a large wooden porch that ran almost the length of the entire building where we could sit and watch all the action going on outside. The doors to the rooms at each end of the porch had windows with wooden slats to allow for controlling the amount of air coming into the rooms.

Opening the door to our room I gasped. A pale yellow floor was surrounded by yellowish-white walls with huge wooden latticed windows covering two sides of the room. Unlike the other monasteries where we were given much-used rainbow-colored quilts and sleeping mats, here we were offered beautiful soft, yellow and white cotton comforters and sleep-ing futons. I couldn't help thinking that Martha Stewart would definitely approve. The color coordination, the attention to aesthetics, the simplic-ity—a single flower here, a small set of stones there—was exquisite.

Best of all, we had a Western-style bathroom with a toilet and a shower. Goodbye outhouses. Goodbye filth. We had arrived in Tusita heaven (a Buddhist heaven where all desires are met).

Lunging for the shower, I washed myself and my robes, scrubbing both raw, not caring if the robes dried in time for our next excursion (they didn't). By that point wearing wet clothes was no big deal. They were clean. Following a lunch of rice, tea, soup, and vegetables (mostly in the form of kimchi) we hiked all around the area, returning in time for evening service. Listening to a thousand nuns chant together sent chills up my spine. It seemed as though we had landed in a field of angels and we were sitting right in the middle of them. Then came the treat of treats. After the service two young nuns walked onto a square outdoor platform in the middle of the campus. There was a huge drum about ten feet in diameter. The nuns took their positions on each side of the drum. It looked like they were meditating. Suddenly WHAM! WHAM! WHAM! WHAM! A huge powerful drumbeat started. It got faster. Louder. Faster. Louder. First one nun. Then, without missing a beat, the second one took over. WHAM! WHAM! WHAM! WHAM! The whole valley was filled with the sound.

Watching the women bashing the drum with all their strength under a full moon was better than, oh I don't know, being the only person at a Grateful Dead concert. Words don't exist to describe the sheer power of the experience. Even our hearts beat to their rhythms.

Following morning practice and breakfast the next day, watching the nuns go about their business, I felt comforted somehow. The earth has some pretty strong hands holding it up after all, hidden in the darnedest places.

Chapter Eleven

P'arang Sunim

Journal entry: September 20, 1999, Seoul

"The longer and more arduous the trip, the more your heart has a chance
to open up until finally, in a moment of utter exhaustion, you realize
that's all of you that is left—the heart part. Your mind has disappeared—
the one that judges and gets mad and worries and thinks and fantasizes.
Instead you are in love with your life, whatever it is. And *the whole world*
is your family with the earth playing the lead role as universal nest, one
you are thrilled (!) to share with all takers. I almost forgot. You'll also lose
ten pounds without even trying. Maybe more."

As we were headed for the pilgrimage finish line, Sunim started to
prod at us in a totally different way. He was gentle but still prodding, ever
prodding. Forget sleeping—there wasn't time. Just let go of everything.
Everything. We knew we would survive—we had faced humidity, filth,
typhoons, sheer physical exhaustion, and even death. All that mattered
was letting go of it all. Just staying in now.

As we were leaving Unmunsa, Sunim said to me, still gentle,
"P'arang, if you like you'll be able to fly." I just laughed and went back
to chanting. Sunim looked at me hard. "Do more. Do extra practice."

Okay.

I decided that the extra practice would be to stay hunkered down
with "what is it?" It was an old familiar *hwadu* and it had taken all sorts
of shapes and forms during the trip. Sometimes it was "just this," some-

times it was chanting, sometimes it was rushing, singing, eating. Now "what is it?" reverted back to great questioning. "What is it?" "What is it?" "What is it?" I locked into it, like a dog with a hard-won bone. I vowed to stick with the questioning until my feet touched ground in Chicago. It wasn't easy. My brain wanted to go home in the worst way possible. It wanted to plan meals, and to think about moving to a smaller place. It wanted to make a list of all the school supplies my daughter Jamie would need for school the week we got back. Instead I stuck with "What is it?"

It was great.

The next day a typhoon hit, raining so hard we couldn't see our feet. No big deal. We just climbed down the last mountain to the sound of chanting following us down.

For some reason the only thoughts that seeped through my practice were about Ananda, Buddha's attendant. Out of the blue I found myself thinking about his life story and what it would have been like to live in Buddha's time with him. I thought about how if Ananda and I ever made it into the same time and place zone, we would be best friends. I'm sure of it. As Buddha's key attendant for thirty-five years, Ananda stuck with Buddha through thick and thin. When Buddha's cousin Devadatta decided that it was time to kill the Buddha once and for all—he had already tried a couple of times—and set loose a drunk elephant hurtling toward Buddha, Ananda was the only disciple who didn't dive out of the way. I just knew he would have defended me when Donny Beverly was beating me up in the third grade and he would have broken down every door to help me when I was being stalked. He would have told Sunim to back off when he was yelling at us and he would have scolded me to get a grip when I overreacted.

In fact he was the world's best nag. Ananda just wouldn't drop it when Buddha told him women couldn't be disciples. Buddha finally gave in to Ananda's argument that if women could be enlightened then surely they could be disciples. Ananda gave up everything for Buddha, even his own shot at full enlightenment while Buddha was still alive. To take the time for practice would have meant leaving Buddha, which he was unwilling to do. When Buddha was dying Ananda worried on behalf of all of us. Did Buddha have anything else to teach? Had he missed anything that had to be passed on? Ananda became a real basket case. What about a successor? He begged Buddha to name somebody. Buddha said no. Was Buddha sure he had covered everything that needed to be covered? "I have hidden nothing, Ananda."

But Ananda wouldn't stop. Was Buddha sure? I can just picture Buddha, trying to focus on dying, sick to his stomach from eating food that had gone bad. Finally, this:

"Be islands unto yourselves, refuges unto yourselves, seeking no external refuges, with the Dhamma as your island, the Dhamma as your refuge." (Ayya Khema, *Be an Island: The Buddhist Practice of Inner Peace,* Wisdom Publications, Boston, 1999, p. xv)

Ananda shut up at last.

Oh my God! That was it! That was what the Diamond Sutra and Faithmind and everything else had been trying to teach. Enlightenment is an inside job. Literally. Be a lamp unto yourself. That's what Sunim taught me. Not to depend on anything, even him. Instead, depend on my own sincere heart. He had been saying that to me for years. But I hadn't listened. I wanted him to be my island, to be the perfect teacher, holding my hand as I took baby steps from one shore to the next. Instead he threw me off an emotional cliff. And holding onto the last branch of my own beliefs, my own "this is how it's supposed to be" I almost missed the point of the whole pilgrimage, I was so busy being furious so much of the time.

Everything we need is in our own sincere hearts.

All the wisdom, all the courage, all the compassion it takes to fall into our own enlightenment and everyone else's. The whole world's in fact. It's all Buddha.

Hilarious, this ego thing.

Getting back to Seoul after weeks in the mountains we plunged into doing chores from dawn to dusk. We had to collect books from all the places we'd left them, and buy thank-you gifts for everyone who had kept the temple in Ann Arbor running in our absence. And most important, we scrubbed ourselves and our robes clean so people would be able to sit next to us on the plane without holding their noses for the entire trip.

As we were leaving our room in the Seoul temple for the airport, Sunim looked at me hard. I thought he was going to yell at me one last time since we had been arguing about how many bags Haju and I could take through customs. Many of the books, clothes, and a couple of vases that had been given to him had been packed into three enormous suitcases. Each one was too heavy for either Haju or me to pick up. Plus he wanted each of us to carry a boxed vase home for him. All without paperwork since they were gifts.

I was fit to be tied. How would we get everything out of the airport at the other end? What would we say to customs if they asked us what was inside each bag? Since Haju and I hadn't packed them, the truth was we didn't know.

Three times I asked for paperwork. Three times Sunim said, "Don't worry." After a while we stopped arguing. It wasn't worth the energy. In the silence I picked up my backpack and one of the boxed vases. Moving for the door Sunim caught my eye. "Well, P'arang," he said. "You went into the mountains a dharma teacher. And you came out a Sunim."

P'arang Sunim. Hmmm. I pretty much ignored him, still focused on the customs issue. P'arang Sunim. There he was giving me his blessing. Telling me I was ready to go back into the marketplace as a full Zen monk.

Maybe. If I am it took everything we had. For both of us. Three years of training in thirty days. I suddenly remembered going to visit a psychic in the second year I was in the seminary. It was an act of sheer desperation in such a hellish year that, like Ananda, I just had to try to understand

144

what the heck was going on so I could keep going. Had I mistakenly landed in some secret hell realm? My karmic punishment for stealing candy at Woolworth's when I was six because I had lost my lunch money? Weren't Zen masters supposed to be kind, I asked her. Weren't they supposed to be filled with compassion? Anger free? How could they shout at their own students? How could they correct and correct and correct without end? Sunim was a shouter. He wouldn't let any mistake slide. Everything was correction, correction, correction. He was the Energizer Bunny reconstituted as a never-ending correcting Zen master. Help!

The psychic looked at me kindly.

"He's just doing his job."

Yup. He did his job.

Customs never did ask us what was in our boxes. They just waved us on, the way Sunim said they would. Waved us back into the land of pizza and children and cars and air pollution. Home.

I had to stop myself from kissing the ground when I walked out of the terminal into the windy Chicago afternoon.

Chapter Twelve

Pleas
from the Mountains

Journal entry: September 20, 1999, on the plane home

"I did it! I stayed to the end. It took everything I had and then some. Mostly it took surrendering to Buddha and my practice *over and over ad nauseam*. But it worked. Those monks were amazing… They have so much clarity in their eyes and mannerisms—utter awareness. My favorites (Oh good grief. I still have favorites. There is work yet to be done!) were the ones with the great senses of humor. How lucky to be content with each day. I'll miss their energy and their giggles and the sheer sanity of their words. Probably as much as I've missed grilled cheese sandwiches and orange juice for the past month.

"It will be so nice to not have people staring at us all the time and holding their noses because of the smell which has ripened into sort of a urinal-laced-sour-meat-odor. It will be nice to grow hair again and to have a bath when I want one, and a real bed. It will be nice to be home."

When *Stumbling Toward Enlightenment* came out I had no idea what to expect. Would my mother be the only person who read it cover to cover? Would any of my friends still talk to me? Would the publishers ask for their advance back? Would Oprah call? Within weeks I started to get letters, all but one thanking me, from people who had stumbled into the book, some literally. Bookstores called to ask if I would be willing to do a book signing—I said yes to those within a two-hours-on-a-good-day drive.

One was Schulers in Lansing, Michigan, a wonderful store with a loyal following. My instruction was to read a couple of passages from the book and then sit at a lovely antique desk to sign copies. Halfway through the reading I stopped and decided to just chat and take questions, figuring that they could all read anything I might read since it was all in the book, after all. I talked about being in the seminary, about some of my more colorful mistakes, and about how spiritual life has changed my life completely, for better and worse.

After about twenty minutes of this, I asked if anyone had any questions. There was a woman sitting in the front row who had started to frown from the moment I opened my mouth. She instantly stuck her hand up. I nodded in her direction. She stood up. "I thought monks were supposed to be quiet and wise." I looked at her. "This *is* quiet and wise for me. You should have seen me before." The answer seemed to work since the frown disappeared.

Then I turned around and did the same thing to the monks in Korea. Like her, I expected them all to be quiet and wise, eyes down, sort of like a Zen rendition of the pictures of Jesus I had seen as a small child. Walking in slow motion of course, doing everything delicately, with a half smile, a barely visible aura around their heads. Instead, wild monks, grinning monks, yelling monks, frowning monks, look-into-my-eyes monks, glowing monks, glowering monks.

And eccentric, thy name is monkhood. Whew. Stories of eccentric monks could have filled the pages of all our journals. Here's just one. During one of the periods when Japan controlled Korea (1910–1945) there was a big split among the monks. The ones who capitulated to the Japanese became *kyo* or sutra monks. The meditation monks, on the other hand, often illiterate, did not. This made them susceptible to everything from person-to-person crimes to becoming tools of the Japanese government.

One of the few meditation monks to become an abbot decided, during a New Year's service, that he had had enough of Japanese rule. Right in the middle of the service he jumped up and shouted at the governor general, "If you keep doing (what you are doing) you will end up in the worst hell!" With that he walked right out of his own ceremony. The governor general was understandably furious but hesitated to have the monk executed because he knew it would probably start riots and feed the growing nationalism that was festering in the mountains.

A few days later the same monk was invited to give a public dharma talk. At the event a Japanese official knocked him over as he walked past. This was a great insult. The monk ignored him, only saying that the official should be as good picking people up as he was knocking them down. But his tension grew until finally, in a room full of meditation monks, he shouted, "We all know we're ignorant!" Then he drew a short horizontal line on a piece of paper, the symbol for the number one. He showed it to the meditation monks, "Can you explain this to me?"

The monks, figuring it was a *hwadu* question testing their level of awakeness, stayed silent. And he let out a roar. "You motherfucker sons of cocksuckers! You can't even answer a simple question!" Out he stormed leaving behind jaws that dropped open and have probably never quite closed to this day.

The way Sunim explained the monk's behavior went something like this: Eventually you grow out of the forms—the hierarchy, the rituals, the here's-how-we-do-its. Wonhyo was a clear example of this with his ancient antics and village-to-village storytelling. He embodied what the sutras try to teach, nondualism, pure "just this"ness.

All of the monks had something to teach us, Sunim said.

The lessons weren't anything I could have imagined. For example, there were no formal presentations of Haju to the Zen masters after all.

Instead it was more like she and I were along for the ride. Looking back I suspect that it was enough of a shock to see two women dressed in monk's garb for some of the older monks. And, frankly, they appeared to be generally more interested in learning about the West and Sunim's work here than lecturing us on the dharma. So most of our visits were question and answer sessions focused on Sunim. So little of our conversations were directed at Haju and me that I didn't bother to write down most of what was said.

On the other hand there were moments that made all the hardships of Korea worthwhile. Mostly they revolved around watching how the monks interacted with other people with grace and humor and kindness. Several were in the process of actively dying. One spent most of our visit asking about the United States because he is planning to be reborn somewhere in the Midwest. Beyond the exposure of how an enlightened life plays out, the monks offered powerful insights into our own culture and made the pilgrimage, in the end, the trip of a lifetime. Highly recommended for Westerners convinced that they've already reached their spiritual heights—guaranteed to leave the ego component of who you are bleeding on the side of whatever road you happen to be travelling. No big deal, they'd say.

As we were moving out of the mountains toward Yosu we spent a long day of hiking, only to top it off with a long meeting with a social worker monk who invited us to join him on a night walk along a pitch black mountain path. Only the sound of the river gave us clues about direction. There was no source of light, the trees were so thick. Suddenly we came to a clearing and a long low building that looked like a Korean version of a Motel 6 plunked down in the middle of a mountain path. Go figure. It looked like there were about a dozen rooms. Some of them had lights on; one or two emitted the sound of a radio or television. We walked beside the building, trying (and failing on my part) not to look inside the open doors.

Without warning, a surprise invitation put us face to face with an impish 86-year-old "retired" Zen master. When we walked into his room the first thing he did was insist that Haju and I arm wrestle him. First Haju lost, then I did. Suddenly he turned and stared at Haju like a ferocious tiger. "Show me your practice!" he shouted. She whacked the floor. He shouted, "No!" She shouted, "Ho!" He grabbed his teaching stick, a long staff, and acted out that he was about to hit her. Sunim intervened. "Grab his stick." She did and hit the floor three times. He looked at her, still the tiger. "Why did you do that?" She put her camera on her head.

Suddenly we were in the middle of a thousand-year-old dharma combat. He was interviewing us, looking for the strength of our practice. Had we given up our egos, our thinking minds? Were we living spontaneously, driven by our hearts? Or were we mere tourists, dressed in monk's gray?

I sat grinning in the background.

He looked at both of us. "All the nuns make sounds and do things others have done. The point is to demonstrate your own authentic mind, your own heart. How do you do that?"

I grabbed the bowl of grapes on the floor and carefully but quickly put it on the desk in front of him. He shouted, "No!" I shouted, "Yaiiiiii!" He threw us out. Interview over.

What a blast!

But then we met up with the monk of monks.

Journal entry: September 10, 1999, Songgwangsa

"His room is 8 feet by 20 feet. It's all he needs. A straw mat with a room-sized pad under it covers most of the floor. There are two soccer balls. On one wall, nothing. On two others paper-covered doors with windows above them. On the last wall a horizontal bamboo pole. Hanging on it: one robe, two kasas, one pair of green athletic socks. Above the pole, a huge straw hat.

"In one corner of the room are three pink blankets. One of them is pale pink satin with lace. In the second corner, a telephone with lots of special buttons on it. The third corner is home to a small pile of clothes. His tea set, complete with a small pot for boiling water, fills the last. Everything he owns, except for a small box of valuables, is in our sight."

At 83, the abbot of Hwaomsa expects to live to be 100. When we showed up at his door he proceeded to invite us in and then lay on top of one of the soccer balls, belly up, and rolled all over it with his body. The ball moved up and down his back while he kicked his legs in the air like an overturned turtle. I tried not to laugh. Almost choked from the effort.

Looking in our direction while he was rolling, he made a simple statement. "Expensive exercise equipment is unnecessary when you have a soccer ball." With that, he picked up the bigger soccer ball and, lying on it, back to the ceiling, rolled all over the floor again. Grin. Then he sat on the ball and bounced around for a couple of minutes. My mouth had fallen open from a combination of delight and utter disbelief. After a few bounces he rubbed his head all over the ball, smiled, and asked if we would like to have tea with him.

You bet.

It was strong green tea. Since we had been up since 3 A.M. per usual, and it was afternoon, we gulped it down. The abbot immediately started to boil a second pot of water for another batch.

While we waited for the water to boil he launched into a monologue in Korean that lasted one and a half hours. No topic was left untouched. First he talked about his own life and the state of Buddhism in the world. (Not great. Lots of persecution in Asia. Lots of harassment by Christians in Korea.) He announced that the Dalai Lama was not fully enlightened and that the problem with monks in Tibet, Thailand, and the United States is that we talk too much. "That's part of the Dalai Lama's problem," he added. Also, "Americans make lousy monks." He was right. I already knew that by Korean standards we make lousy monks. In my whole life I can think of only three people who would happily get up every day at 3 A.M. and spend a whole day doing manual work, chanting, sutra study, and sitting until 9 or 10 P.M. With *exactly* the same foods at each meal. For a lifetime. No television, no email, no bathtubs. It's a tough path. I am not one of those three persons. Give up *Will and Grace?* I don't think so.

The abbot watched us digest his words. We were all quiet for a while. Then he smiled. We were sincere spiritual travelers who were looking for a middle way for the next century. Okay. He took us on a tour of the temple grounds, randomly stopping to look at us and smile. The closer I got the more I felt like I was in love, only there wasn't anyone I was in love with. In his room I was so in love I blushed. But as soon as I walked away, it was gone.

Go figure.

We visited yet another wise man. Pophung Sunim is a 68-year-old renowned scholar of Japanese scriptures who has traveled the world. Every time he thought of a topic that might be of interest to us he would walk into the next room, where there were books floor to ceiling along the walls and piles as tall as he was in the middle of the room, and find one on the subject to give to us. We ended up with eight I think.

I asked Pophung how to help an authentic Buddhism to grow in the West. His answer was long and complicated but roughly boiled down to four things. First, we need to put all of our effort into *bodhicitta* ("mind of enlightenment" in Sanskrit). We need to aspire, with all the energy we can muster, to enlightenment for the sake of helping others. Our compassion would fuel our effort, he promised. We needed to keep going until we could directly perceive—all the time—the true nature of phenomena, which is emptiness. (A pretty clumsy way of saying this is that everything changes all the time, that in the end nothing has a permanent essence. Let's both work on this one together, shall we?)

Second, we need to learn the scriptures, starting with the core teachings of Buddha. Then move out from there. The scriptures provide guideposts and advice that's deeper than any Dear Abby or Dr. Laura response to the tough questions.

The third piece of advice was a theme that kept coming up during the pilgrimage. We must try to not get caught up in money and sex and all their related attachments—television, movies, Internet sites—where we know better. I sat there thinking that it's probably a good thing he hasn't been to the United States in a while to see how caught up we've really become in all this stuff. Many of us can't get to sleep without hearing how the stock market has done. A friend of mine told me that people are flocking to 12-step sex addiction programs because Internet pornography is taking our sex addictions to a new level. All the while, kids still go hungry all over the world every day. You just have to wonder how many of the world's problems we could solve if we all swore off sex for a month and turned all that pent-up energy toward solving some of the "intractable" problems we face. Wouldn't *that* be something?

His last piece of advice: Endure and persevere. Just keep going. Just keep holding all things as precious. Just keep seeing Buddha in every pair of eyes. Endurance counts for a lot in a tradition that has now withstood over a thousand years of pummeling. We have to keep our faith mind (*sinsim*) strong, to believe in ourselves, and in the power of our practice. That way, he promised, we wouldn't fall backwards. In that way we would be able to embrace the whole world, to be real bodhisattvas instead of bodhisattva look-alikes. We would be Samantabhadra.

We would be Samantabhadra?

Spelling aside, Samantabhadra is one of the key bodhisattvas in Mahayana Buddhism. He is honored not just as a protector but *the* protector of everyone who teaches the dharma. Buddhists think of him, assuming they know about him, as the embodiment of pure wisdom, the true wish-fulfilling jewel.

Here's a sample of what he can pull out of people:

THE ASPIRATION OF SAMANTABHADRA

By the power of my faith in the deeds
of Samantabhadra,
I prostrate and present
vast and unequalled offerings
to each of the victorious Buddhas.

I confess every type of wrong that I
have done in thought, word, or deed,
under the influence of desire, anger,
or ignorance...

May whatever small amount of virtue I
may have gained from prostrating, offering,
confessing, rejoicing, requesting, and
beseeching be dedicated to attaining
perfect enlightenment.

May I perform all the deeds of enlightenment
and remember all my lives in all states of
existence. And in all my lives, after death,
migration, and rebirth, may I always embrace
spiritual life.

(For a full copy of "The Aspiration of Samantabhadra" visit
www.flex.com/~jai/articles/samantabhadra.html)

Okay!

* * *

By the time we had returned to Seoul, then we had met monks, monks, and more monks, from the young eager ones to old timers preparing to shed the skin of this lifetime. We had sat at the feet of monks who will be remembered as great saints and spent afternoons with a few who may be remembered as scoundrels, and even a "bad" monk or two thrown in for spiciness. Mostly our interaction was conversation. Words. Here, what we got was enlightenment in action. The minute I saw him, my brain named him Santa Claus Sunim (not that he had a hair on his head!).

He was middle aged, maybe in his late forties. Ordinary looking. Nice. A married monk with a child. He had started three temples, all centered around Quanseum Posal, the Bodhisattva of Compassion, and all manner of social service projects—practically a country's worth and he was just one monk. One of the projects is a huge building—maybe five stories high—which houses a kindergarten, day-care center, elder care, health clinic, and lots of crafts programs all mixed together. When we went into the building there was a clashing and banging sound as when all of your pots and pans fall out of the cupboard at once. The sound kept repeating. I thought I was imagining it, but everyone else had the same am-I-hearing-things look. We made our way up the stairs to visit the different programs and discovered where the sounds were coming from—a room full of little old ladies flailing away at drums and having the time of their lives. A few doors down, we heard singing. There a handful of people were practicing old Korean folk songs for a local holiday.

In a nearby day-care building we saw what you would expect— adorable pictures and paintings and crafts—as well as surprises such as a miniature tearoom where the children are taught "the way of tea" and an organic garden surrounding the building, cared for by preschoolers. The monk explained that there are two overriding values they instill in the children: 1) respect your parents; and 2) love nature (so they'll protect it as adults). People would sidle up to Santa Claus monk everywhere we went and he had hugs for everyone—even a teeny elderly woman he immediately scolded for having had some alcohol. The love in his eyes for her was palpable. Every day, all day long he runs those programs with a gentleness and caring that probably even Santa would envy.

One monk moved me to tears. Actually he was a former monk, now an artist. We spent the better part of a morning with him while he showed Sunim pictures he had painted and pretended that he wasn't paying any attention to me and Haju. After several hours of tea and fruit slices he walked right up to the two of us as we stood by the front door to leave. I was taken aback, partly because he was a big man—think football player—and partly because he was so close to us. He could have kissed Haju without leaning into her—that close. He just stared at both of us for a few seconds. I stood there without a clue about what to expect. By coming so close to us he was breaking all the protocol rules I knew and probably more that I (happily) didn't know. Then he grabbed our hands. I figured, at that point, we're all going to hell with all the rules we've broken by now so I held his hand back. I think Haju did as well although I was mostly so dumbfounded by his gesture that I could only look at his face.

Tears filled his eyes.

"Practice," he said. "Stay with it. You'll protect heaven and earth if you do." He was begging us. He was begging for all of our lives, that we not lose them to the *samsara* (the indefinitely repeated cycles of birth and death caused by karma) of fast foods, the Internet, our bank accounts, and sex on the brain. He was begging us to trade in any leftover ego-based thinking for wide open kindness where every day we can look up at the clouds knowing that at least one wild-eyed, chuckling monk is looking at the same clouds, wishing us well, and probably thinking, "Who were those women anyway?"

157

Flying home, I mostly thought about the monks and nuns—the glowy ones and what was inside of them that kept them going through thick and thin. It had to be *sinsim*, or faith mind. Not so much a faith in themselves, but faith that enlightenment is there for the taking. And with it the best kind of tranquility—not running away, not running toward. They knew how to be with whatever was right smack in front of them without the small-scale "I" trying to control every little thing. Dainin Katagiri taught, years ago, that tranquility is impossible if our life is embossed with the small-scale "I" because in that place there is always some irritation and restlessness.

I'll say.

That was it. Their small-scale "I"s were gone, or mostly gone. And there was a solidness about them I couldn't pinpoint—the Buddhist teacher Ayya Khema calls it mind solitude. They just plain didn't care if we were impressed with them or liked them or whatever. They were just who they were, serving tea, talking about running a temple, cleaning, sweeping the walks, or sneaking us clean socks.

Looking back, I could have jumped, danced, cheered, made banners, and paraded them and I am certain—to a monk—that the biggest reaction would have been a smile, that Buddha half smile you see in all the pictures and on so many statues. And I'm sure I could have yelled obscenities and called each one an antichrist and the reaction would have been exactly the same: the Buddha smile. *Sinsim* rocks.

Journal entry: September 15, 1999, Unmunsa

"Last night I couldn't stand how filthy my meditation clothes were so I washed them. This morning still wet. I put them on anyway. They are beginning to feel like my own P'arang blanket. They've become the shape of my body. Here's the metaphor. It's like washing a shirt: You can get it clean in lots of ways. You can gently rub it with soap and slowly but surely work the dirt out or you can put soap all over the shirt and beat the dirt and grime right out of it. This trip has been the latter. The dirt and grime have been beaten right out of us."

To summarize the journey:

1. Most moving moment: when the big monk held our hands and cried with us.

2. Hardest moment: being exhausted at the indigo farm.

3. Best practice moment: on the mountain with the nun doing kido practice—amazing in the extreme—bragging rights if I was into spiritual capitalism.

4. Best quote: "In pure mindfulness everything is poetry," from our own Haju Sunim.

5. Favorite person: too many to name; mostly the artist monks and posalnims.

6. Funniest moment: the old monk rolling all over the soccer ball, laughing out loud in the extreme.

7. Lessons taking home: just surrender. (I'm doomed to dharma. Fly a white flag and get over it.)

8. Biggest surprise gift—a three-way tie: 1) being in the presence of the monks, 2) major life issues somehow resolved, 3) clarity about what matters.

9. Favorite place: bathhouse in Pusan.

10. Favorite food—a tie: fried pancakes with strips of vegetables in them, hot or cold, and the Korean ice-cream treat at Don't Worry Café.

11. Least favorite food: seaweed soup.

12. Would have brought had I known: insect repellant and sneakers that wouldn't fall apart.

13. One-word description of the trip: relentless.

May all beings be free from ever having to climb a mountain in a typhoon.

POSTSCRIPT

On September 10, 2000, P'arang Geri Larkin held the first public meditation service at a new temple in the heart of Detroit, Michigan, the Still Point Zen Buddhist Temple, as its guiding teacher. Samu Sunim advised her to remember to "be strict and be a good friend."